MW00630472

HAUNTING BRITISH COLUMBIA

HAUNTING
BRITISH COLUMBIA

GHOSTLY TALES FROM THE PAST

MIKE McCARDELL

HARBOUR
PUBLISHING

Harbour Publishing Co. Ltd.
P.O. Box 219, Madeira Park, BC, V0N 2H0
www.harbourpublishing.com

Cover image by Nick Didlick
Edited by Pam Robertson
Text design by Roger Handling
Printed and bound in Canada

Harbour Publishing acknowledges the support of the Canada Council for the Arts, the Government of Canada, and the Province of British Columbia through the BC Arts Council.

Library and Archives Canada Cataloguing in Publication

Title: Haunting British Columbia : ghostly tales from the past / Mike McCardell.
Names: McCardell, Mike, 1944- author.
Identifiers: Canadiana (print) 2021029244X | Canadiana (ebook) 20210292458 | ISBN 9781550179552 (hardcover) | ISBN 9781550179569 (EPUB)
Subjects: LCSH: British Columbia—History—Anecdotes.
Classification: LCC FC3811.8 .M33 2021 | DDC 971.1—dc23 Cataloguing data available from Library and Archives Canada
ISBN 9781550179552 (cloth)
ISBN 9781550179569 (ebook)

DEDICATION

It is hard, and it is easy, to say thank you.

Hard because there are so many. Easy because they deserve more than just thanks.

A while ago I went to CTV News after a long time somewhere else. I was an outsider. I was, still am, older.

They could have stood back and let me come and go, pass by, without getting involved.

Instead, all of them were good and patient and encouraging. More than in words, they were welcoming. If you have ever gone into a new place and not gotten welcomed you know what this means.

From the news director to the producers, the writers, the impossible-to-do job of coordinating cameras and assignments—which would destroy a weak person—to the directors and anchors and web writers and assignment editors and engineers and audio technicians and security. And people who do things where I do not know what they are doing, and the reporters, and those who turn tiny microchips into big pictures, and the fellow who fixes the computers—which is like on-the-job open heart surgery—and those who clean the bathrooms. Thank you. But there are too many names.

However, two groups hold me and guide me and help me every day. The camera folks and the editors. I live not only by their work but their dedication—which is a big word—their caring when they say, "One more picture" or "You can say something better than that." The photographers and editors who you never see are the pilots in the life raft of every story every day, including those who were here and are no longer here because of the cruelty of budget cuts. Without them no story. Too many names, not nearly enough ink to say thank you.

This is for you.

Table of Contents

INTRODUCTION

Introductions are supposed to introduce you to something, or someone. But you probably already know me, at least I hope you do.

I revealed my secret life in the book *Haunting Vancouver* a few years ago.

I am a ghost. I lived long ago in BC, and I am still around now. Please don't say you don't believe in ghosts because if I wasn't real how could I be typing this, with a coffee cup alongside, telling you I am real? That's all the proof I can offer.

So I am a true-to-life ghost.

In the earlier book I told you about the headliners of the early city, the ones you grew up hearing about and I lived with: Gassy Jack (bad reputation now but he sold beer and gave birth, accidently, to Vancouver), Joe Fortes (did not own a restaurant but saved lives, which is better than cooking steaks), Emily Carr (who if she saw the Emily Carr University of Art and Design would say, "Whaaatt? How did that happen?").

Now let's turn to some of the others I met during my eternity in this province, which almost became an American state. It was saved by a guy who was good and bad and big and small, like most of us. Let's start with him.

THE BIG STEAL

Sorry, I took a nap.

It is nice when you are dead and get tired. No one notices when you slip away. And the best part of being dead and coming back to life and then sleeping is you don't have to get up and pee.

That used to ruin my sleep. No more. Just sleep.

So I was telling you about things in the past. That is called History. That is the best subject of all. But it is one they ruin in school.

King Whatever, and War Wherever. How about a story? Like just tell a story about something that happened or some nutcase—excuse me, lovable nutcase—who did something and changed everything.

Let us do that. Right now. There will not be a test at the end, so if you want to sleep I won't mind.

I met you, you met me, choose either one, a few books ago. The title was *Haunting Vancouver: A Nearly True History of Vancouver*. The publisher added that word "Nearly," like he did not believe I was real. I wanted to tell him to get real, but then I am a ghost—if he does not believe I am me, I cannot change that.

However, I am real. If I was not, how could I possibly have told you the inside scoop of what really happened with some wild characters who made Vancouver?

As for me, if you really do not know, I was a combat engineer, a Sapper, one of the fellows sent in 1858 by Queen Victoria to help settle this land, and mostly to keep it out of the hands of America. We succeeded with both of those. There were 160 of us, who could dig and shoot, survey and march, draw blueprints for a town or plan a battle. We were the Royal Engineers, and we could do anything.

By the way, Vickie was one of my favourite people. I got to see her briefly before we sailed away. But one really annoying trait of hers was she ate like a, well, I cannot use an animal comparison but she ate like a commoner.

She would gobble her food as fast as it was put in front of her. That was fine if she was eating alone or with Prince Albert, who she really, really loved. It was a sad ending when he died.

But back to eating. When she had a royal dinner with guests sitting at a long table, well, those poor guests. Vickie of course would be served first and as soon as the plate hit the table her fork would hit the meat.

Gobble, gobble. She would finish before her guests were all served. The ones who did get food in front of them and maybe got a bite to their mouth were lucky because when the Queen put down her fork dinner was over. Everyone's fork had to be down.

Other than that she was sweet. But talking about eating, her son, who became Edward VII, was a super glutton. He ate so much he could not fit inside his jackets and his bottom button always had to be undone. That is the reason men still today do not button the bottom button on their jackets. We are all so easily influenced.

She also blamed him for the death of Albert.

I want to remind you that history can be taught boringly: in 1901 Edward became King following the death of Victoria.

Or it can be taught with screams and blame. It was thus: Edward, whose nickname was Bertie, and how can you be taken seriously as a king in waiting with the name Bertie, liked women, especially married ones. When he was away having yet another liaison his mother was upset and his father went off to bring him back. But Albert returned with typhoid, which killed him.

Victoria never forgave her son. So she kept him waiting to be King longer than any other male heir in the history of the royal family—except for

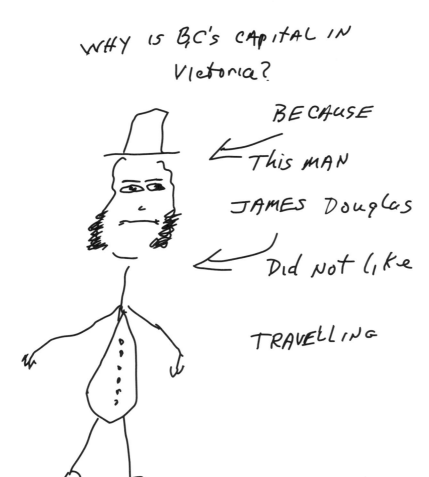

WHY IS BC's CAPITAL IN Victoria?

BECAUSE

This MAN

JAMES Douglas

Did Not like

TRAVELLING

the current prince in waiting, Charles, whose mother seems not to trust him either.

Enough, enough! I want to tell you the story of why the capital of British Columbia is far away and hard to get to, unless of course you live there, which many do not.

You know the capital was New Westminster. You do know that, right? When we Sappers arrived we picked a spot from which we could blast out of the water any American war ships that might be coming up the Fraser River.

They would do us no good, and we would welcome them with pounding cannons. You know that old saying: Don't Mess With New West.

Our camp grew quickly into the city of New Westminster. It was the capital of the colony, and it had everything a capital would need. It had a government building and it had bars, and it had a real estate office, and it had bars, and it had a blacksmith shop and bars and across the street another bar.

It was perfect as the seat of government.

But then the Colony of British Columbia, which was this gigantic hunk of land, united with the Colony of Vancouver Island.

And the problem was, the fellow who wound up in charge of the whole thing lived in Victoria.

He was James Douglas. When you talk about giants, he was. Politically, physically, mentally and with bravery to match, he was made for the job.

But again, he lived in Victoria and he hated waiting for the ferry. Who doesn't?

And when the ferry came it had sails, so he had to wait for the tide to start going out before he could go. That was the only way to get a ship moving. And if there was no wind he had to wait while watching the sun go down.

"Am I going to do this every time someone calls a meeting?"

I heard him say that because I was up on deck with him. My job after the army was as a newspaper reporter and I was just covering another boring, tedious, endless political trip.

When we got to the other side there was the wagon and a horse. We plodded along Kingsway, which we Sappers had built just to get folks to New Westminster.

As we passed some of the used buggy shops he whispered to me, "I am going to change this."

I thought, here is a story about to unfold.

Something else I have to tell you. I did not have a camera. There is a picture of my wife, Mary, and I, but that was done by a professional.

So I developed a little way of remembering what I was witnessing when I covered an event. I got a quill off a goose. Yes, those Canada geese that keep the grass so healthy have been around a long time. And they have great quill feathers, which are perfect for writing.

And I got some ink.

And:

ME, Jock Linn, sketching events As They happened

NO I AM NOT = AN ARTIST — NO Kidding

I only use stick Figures

Draw me!
Draw me!

But it is better then ~~For~~ Forgetting

Anyway, back to the Big Steal. That is what I secretly called moving the capital from New West to Vic. It was corruption at its finest. And the Godfather of the heist was that beautiful man James Douglas. You just never know.

Douglas never smiled. I've seen lots of pictures of him and not a crack in his look of "I've got you and you don't have me. Don't cross me." Scary. But on the other hand he was, and excuse me for using this comparison, he was the George Washington of British Columbia.

He fit the picture. He was perfect for the role. He was Big. No, he was REALLY BIG. Forget the measurements, he looked down on everyone. And he was powerful, strong, and well, that all helps when you want to keep America from stealing your land.

As mentioned many times, he wrote to Queen Vickie asking her to claim the land that would be BC for herself before the American gold miners and the politicians behind them did it.

And she did. And that's why I am here. It worked. It was brilliant. One letter made this land our land, thanks in no small part to me and my fellow Sappers.

But you see, here's a problem. As I said, James Douglas was chief of the Colony of Vancouver Island. Which is a nice place if you don't mind the trouble of getting there.

The Colony of Vancouver Island was this big hunk of beautiful land across the water from the gigantically much larger and more beautiful Colony of British Columbia.

But in 1858 the two colonies married and became one. It was a sweet ceremony, but the best man, James Douglas, was not happy. As I said, he was never happy, but this time he was REALLY not happy. And that is because the capital of both, which were now one, was made to be New Westminster.

"Darn."

James Douglas said that. I know. I heard him.

That would mean a ferry trip every time any document had to be signed, or some silly young politician wanted to say something he thought was brilliant, and it wasn't.

The lineups, the tide, the cancellations, the reservations, the Sunshine Breakfasts when they ran out of bacon. "No," he said. "This can't go on."

And then the words: "I'm going to change this." He said it while on the boat. He said it again on Kingsway, when he complained about the potholes.

"Hey," I wanted to say, "I built that road. Don't complain." But I didn't.

A truth in life is that people complain about things that others have spent back-breaking months building. They think of themselves, and never, no never, think about the people who did the work. A rough road is better than no road.

Enough. No more whining.

His idea was to have a civilized way of deciding where the capital should be. This is how I recorded it in my notebook:

William Cox was from England. We should always write that in upper case, he was from ENGLAND. Good stock. Okay, he was once thrown out of the government assembly for acting like a child. And as a judge he once ordered a business dispute settled by a footrace. But still, good stock.

On the other side, William Franklin. From Ireland. Lower case Ireland. Potatoes, and all that stuff. Franklin was a nice guy who was a good speaker, but he drank too much.

And the moderator of the debate?

James Douglas said the person best suited was: "My son-in-law!"

John Helmcken, that is. He made money in lumber that others cut and sawed and packaged. He was like many industrial leaders. If he had some money to invest, others would make it grow.

John said to his father-in-law: "I will make you proud."

Prior to the debate there was a friendly lunch. Fish and chips, burgers

LET'S HAVE A DEBATE ON MOVING THE capital to Victoria.

HIS IDEA

That's civilized

ON ONE side
william Cox

MY FRIEND.
HE loves Victoria.

The other side
william Franklin

HATES Victoria

17

and fries, sushi—okay, I am advancing the timeline but not the reason for the lunch. They ate fried pork and bread, and had a tiny touch of whiskey.

"Let's have another drink," said Cox, the one who wanted Victoria to win.

"OK!" said Franklin

"LET'S HAVE ANOTHER-y said HELMCKEN

'OK' SAID Franklin AND ANOTHER AND

Right after lunch the debate that would move a capital began.

Cox for Victoria: "Bla, bla, bla, Victoria is the best."

Franklin tried to stand up. He tried again. He took the pages of his speech from his coat pocket and Cox bumped into him. The papers fell to the floor. Cox did the decent thing and picked them up. Then:

And then, quite accidently, Cox bumped into Franklin again and knocked off his glasses. And as he picked them up he popped out the lenses.

"So sorry, old chap, accident you know."

Enter Helmcken into this sad bit of theatre, but he would, as pre-planned, appear to save the day.

"We need a recess," he said.

That sounds good and kind and thoughtful, right?

But when Franklin returned, a bit sober, with new glasses and the pages of his speech in order, Helmcken said: "Sorry, this would be a second speech and you only get one chance."

That was plain rotten.

I swore I could see him looking back at his father-in-law, who was listening to the debate, and I swore again I saw his father-in-law almost smile.

The vote was in favour of Victoria. And that is why James Douglas no longer had to wait for the ferry and why the capital is in Victoria. Theft, corruption and unfairness, what else should a government be founded on?

Sir James Douglas, Governor of the Colony of Vancouver Island and disliker of ferry rides.
Harbour Publishing Archives

MY STORY

It was strange the day one of my editors asked me to write a story about the Sappers.

"But I don't know where you can do your research," he said. "They are fading from memory."

Well, that hurt.

"Maybe I can concentrate on just one of them. That'll make it more personal," I said.

"Good idea."

I like editors who agree with me. But you never know how things will turn out. That simple comment has the most truth of all truths in life. In short: You never know. But I was sure this would be the high point in my career, a shining story of ME, a glowing, factual story of ME. Something to make ME proud. But as I said, you never know how a story will end.

I went straight to Sapperton in New West and to the Fraser View Cemetery. I remember the warm spring day when they lowered my thin wooden casket into the ground. There were tears from my sweet Mary. The girls were holding onto their mother. The boys were in the back of the group and I could not believe it—they looked like they were trying to pick some pockets.

"Stop that!" But they did not hear me.

No one heard me. No one noticed me. Of course not. I was dead and now a newly minted ghost.

But now, a century and a half later, it was winter, and I had come back to look at where I was. And by now others could see and hear me, if I wanted them to.

But I could not find me. There was a little snow on the ground but that should not have been a problem

I expected to see a nice headstone. I heard at the burial that there would be one as soon as some money was raised to buy it. That would not be difficult, I thought.

This is a famous cemetery with at least three super-famous people in it: Gassy Jack, Raymond Burr and me.

Gassy is the fellow who gave birth to Vancouver by running a saloon. He was everyone's hero until folks learned that his Native wife willed her twelve-year-old niece to him when she died. Then suddenly he was a bad guy, but he has a nice big headstone.

And you know Raymond Burr, don't you? How about Perry Mason? Oh, yes, of course.

Raymond Burr, born in New West, went to California to become an actor, joined the US Navy during World War II, got shot in the stomach, survived, and went on to act in almost one hundred movies before making zillions of TV shows as Perry Mason, the lawyer who never lost.

He has a beautiful headstone.

"But where is mine? I know I was buried right about here, near this top end of the grounds. It should be standing tall and proud." But nothing.

So I went to the office, which is a tiny building in the middle of the grounds, and spoke to a fellow with tattoos all over both his arms and asked where Jock Linn was buried.

"The year?"

"1876, April 18, a beautiful day."

He gave me an odd look, then pulled a giant book out of a rack. On its pages were neatly handwritten lists of names and dates and locations.

"Follow me," he said. I followed him back to the spot I remembered.

"Should be here," he said.

He took out a pocket knife, bent down and scraped away the snow, then more than an inch of grass and dirt below it and I could hear scratching.

"Yup, right here," he said.

He scraped away the rest of the ground and there was a slab of dirty mortar about the size of a dishtowel with four letters carved in it.

No first name. No date. No army rank. No praise. Nothing but LINN.

So much for fame.

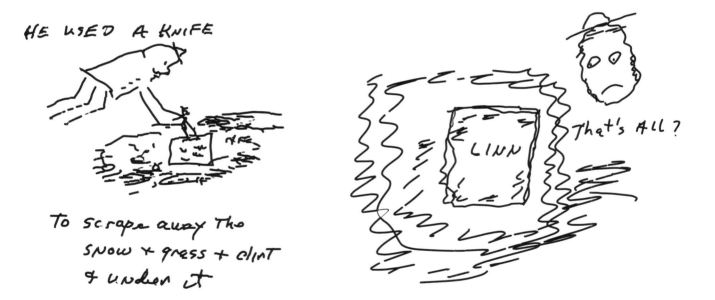

HE USED A KNIFE

To scrape away The snow + gress + dirt + under it

LINN

That's All?

The sad story I wrote for the newspaper was thus:
The Forgotten Sapper, Jock Linn.

Jock Linn was born in Edinburgh. He was a bricklayer, a mason, but when he found himself out of work he joined the army. He was assigned to the Royal Engineers, the Sappers—soldiers who could handle a rifle or a shovel.

He was stationed in Halifax for nine years and there he met Mary Robertson and fell in love. They married and returned to England.

Shortly after Mary and Jock were on a sailing ship heading for the west coast of what would become British Columbia. The trip took six months and during that time of wild seas and cramped quarters Mary had a little girl.

On the crowded, smelly ship they sailed up the Fraser River and stopped where a hill rose up from the water. That would be a good spot to blast apart any American ships that might be coming to lay claim to the land.

And the ships might come because there was a giant army of Americans already here. They were searching for gold and the Sappers' mission was to keep control of them.

The Sappers also had to build roads and structures for a growing new town.

Keeping the peace took all their time. The gold miners had guns and

The real-life Mr. and Mrs. John Linn, namesakes of North Vancouver's misspelled Lynn Creek.
Harbour Publishing Archives

whiskey, along with greed and desperation and rival gangs. It was not good to get between them.

Building roads also took all their time. There was always that forest in the way.

Jock and Mary lived in the Sappers' barracks for eight years, during which time she gave birth to three more girls and two boys.

When the detachment was disbanded in 1867 they moved to the north shore of Burrard Inlet, built a cottage and had a good life. Jock died when he was fifty-five years old.

(What I could not write in the article was that I came back to life on my way to the cemetery. I just woke up inside the coffin, pushed open the top and slipped out when no one was watching. My body was still in there, but I wasn't. Strange how life is. Death too.

As I walked along I realized no one could see me. I was a ghost, don't ask me to explain it.

At the cemetery I watched them lower the coffin, and there were tears and the girls surrounding their mother. It was all very sad. I wanted to say something to Mary, but when I got close she looked right at me and saw nothing.

And I watched my sons doing something that deserved a trip around the back of the barn with me. In just a few minutes I learned a lot about things that I should have noticed when I was able to notice things.

There is a lesson in there about doing what you should do when you can do it.

But I could not write any of this in my article, or I would have been fired.

Another strange thing happened. After I left the cemetery I got my body back. How? Why? Strange things happen all the time and this was my time.

I pulled up my collar and pulled down my hat but no one noticed me anyway. There was only one photo of me and Mary and it was in our cabin and it had been a long time since I was in New West and the crowd had changed. Even though I could be seen I was invisible to this new crowd.)

Back to the article:

Mary and the children continued on. She was now a single mother of six. The girls turned out well, but the boys, well that was another story.

25

One kept getting into trouble and was repeatedly bailed out of jail and his fines paid by his mother. He eventually robbed a store and shot and killed the owner and a helper. He was hanged for that, which was the first hanging in New West.

(Even though they all said they were glad I never knew about it, I did know, and it hurt.)

And his brother cut his own throat. (Even when you are dead death hurts. I can't explain that either, but as you may find out it is true.)

And one daughter died.

In time names changed and the family (like the headstone) faded away except for the honour of naming Lynn Creek and later Lynn Valley after Jock, which someone misspelled.

(The editor asked where I did the research. I told him I knew a very good historian.)

BILLY MINER

I get a misspelled neighbourhood in North Van. He gets a street named after him. You can even see the street sign from my cemetery in New West. That will teach me not to look for medals or stars or even compliments. When you get them they make you feel good. If you don't get them it is meaningless. Don't feel bad.

But as for Billy Miner I have seldom met someone like him who survived the ugliness of hell and came out a good guy.

You probably know people who have lived through really bad things, and others who are wonderfully good, but it is a rare to find the combination. It is hard being honestly good when you've had bad dumped on you.

And it was dumped on Billy.

Of course most of it was his own doing. So why praise him?

He was beaten by a rotten drunk of a father back home in the United States. OK, not his fault. But then he started robbing stagecoaches, just like in those old cowboy movies. His fault.

And he wound up in prison. This part was not in the movies. He was in solitary where the guards would beat him just for the fun of it. Then throw cold water on the concrete floor where he slept, just for the fun of it.

And they would give him bread and water for thirty days, and some-

Billy MINER

MY HERO
The CONVICT

MINER ST.
NEW WESTMINSTER

HONESTLY, HOW MANY
CRIMINALS have a
street named
AFTER THEM?

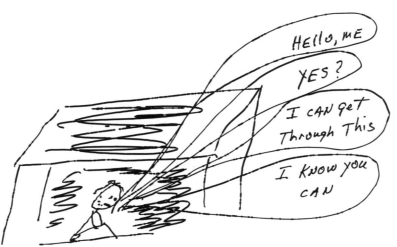

HELLO, ME

YES?

I CAN get
Through This

I KNOW YOU
CAN

times forget the bread. And it was dark and there was nothing to do and the floor was also your bathroom.

And when he got out of solitary there were the older prisoners and sexual brutality.

And when I met him he was a nice guy.

He came to British Columbia in 1904, when he was fifty. He had spent thirty years in prisons. But there were no more stagecoaches, so he robbed trains. It was the only trade he knew.

He had a gun, but he never used it. He was polite, never scary. He did not rob the passengers, only the cash and gold being transported by the Canadian Pacific Railway, which most people hated more than criminals.

You see that picture of me on the cover of this book in the cab of old 374, the CPR engine that first crossed the country? I am celebrating my 200th birthday this year and it is hard to find props to fit that age group. But there

is this old train in a train museum in Vancouver and the publisher said, "Perfect." Publishers say things like that when they think they have an idea.

But if the folks a hundred years ago had seen me in there they would have thrown rotten tomatoes.

The CPR took everything they could get in return for making one skinny little train track across the country. They demanded land far from the steel rails (you'll read about this later when you come to Kits Beach) and they raised the transportation costs for farmers and ranchers while building mansions for their own management team. Some team. You lose, we win.

Anyway, Billy robbed CPR trains, so he was a hero. And he gave money to poor folks. Think Robin Hood. Picture Billy Miner.

The mugshot of legendary train robber Bill Miner, a.k.a. "the Gentleman Bandit," originator of the demand "Hands up!" *Major J.S. Matthews photo, City of Vancouver Archives, AM54-S4-: Port P572*

Eventually, though, he was caught, after a botched train robbery east of Kamloops in 1906. He had been living at the time in Princeton and was sent to prison, to the BC Pen in New West. This time the sentence was life.

However there was a problem for authorities who wanted to humiliate Billy. Waiting at the train station outside the prison were a brass band and thousands of people cheering him.

"Hey Bill! Good luck Bill. We'll wait for you to escape."

"Don't listen to them," the guards said.

And once he was inside there was a little hero worship by the young daughter of the assistant warden. She wanted to convert him. She brought a Bible. She talked to him.

And before long there was a ladder hiding in the weeds near the wall, and Billy was over it and gone.

31

62 year old
Elder statesman
of prisons
+ holdups

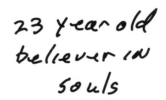

23 year old
believer in
souls

He went down to Georgia and, naturally, went back to robbing trains. And naturally he was caught. And then he died, which naturally happens, but he died peacefully, at the age of sixty-six.

And what naturally happens when a prisoner dies behind bars and has no family is that he is buried in a field for the penniless and unknown.

Not Billy, though. The folks in the town liked, no, loved him so much they paid for his funeral and a handsome gravestone in the main cemetery in town.

What a life. What a nice guy.

And yes, I am just a little jealous that he has something to read on those nights when he cannot sleep.

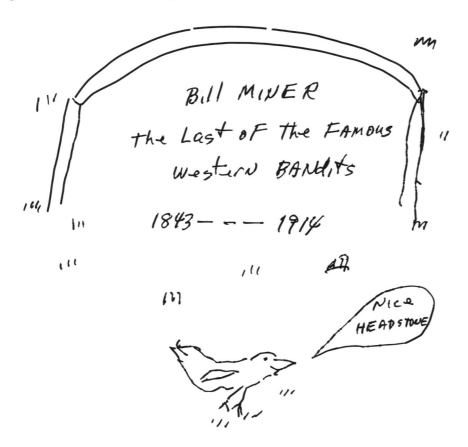

HE HUNG
UPSIDE DOWN

T he newspapers that came out of the tower that is now called the Sun Tower but was the World Tower before that were wild. But something else happened there in 1923 that helped me more than many things in life.

Harry Houdini hung upside down with a rope around his feet and a straitjacket squeezed tightly around his body. He was only two or three storeys up, depending on how you count it, but if he had fallen he would have landed on his head and that would have hurt and it was impossible for him to escape, except of course he did.

I didn't believe it. I went there to watch—along with 20,000 others standing in the street with their heads back and mouths open.

A few minutes before he was hoisted up he climbed onto a platform on the street where members of the Vancouver Police Department dressed him in the straitjacket.

Those things were cruel and unbearable punishment and were used for mentally ill people when they became violent. In my mind the people who put them on others were mentally ill.

Anyway, the poor person's arms were stuffed in sleeves as though you were putting on a jacket backwards. From there on it became torture. Your

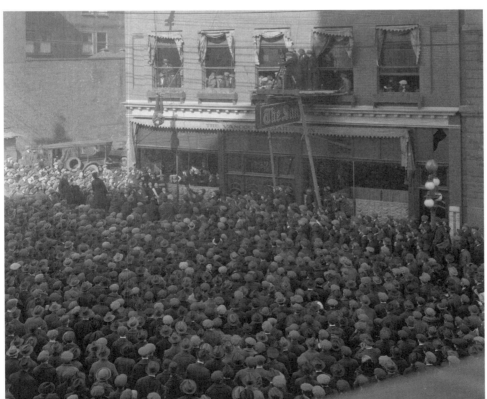

People from all around Vancouver flocked to see Harry Houdini dangling from the corner of the Sun Tower.
W.J. Moore photo, City of Vancouver Archives, AM54-S4-: Port N100

arms were folded across your chest and the straps were pulled tightly. You could not move arms or hands or fingers. You could not breathe, not normal breathing, no pulling in a chestful of air. You could just sip it.

You could not bend or twist. It kept you ramrod straight and the more you struggled the tighter it felt.

I was strapped inside one once to see what it felt like. It was terrifying. No way could Houdini get out of it without a trick, like if someone left some hooks unhooked or a buckle unbuckled. But I was close enough to see the police were putting it on right. I could not figure it out.

Then some constables carried him to the long, hanging rope and tied it around his ankles. They started pulling and the rope came down at their end and at at Houdini's end it went up. Between the police and Houdini a pulley squeaked on each yank.

Houdini was rising feet first. He twitched and contorted, but with my binoculars I could see no loose belts. He could not get out. That was for sure.

The crowd, bigger than any I had seen since Joe Fortes's funeral, was silent.

But in less than two minutes the jacket came off and Houdini held it out and the crowd roared and roared and clapped and shouted.

The rope was lowered and the star was back on the platform bowing and telling everyone to come to his escape-from-handcuffs show that night at the Pantages Theatre. This escape was just a promo for his show, which is where he made his money.

Every seat was filled that evening and Houdini stood on the stage while a constable locked his wrists with regulation police-issue handcuffs, which are impossible to escape from.

Again, I know this to be true because I once had those same cuffs locked on my own wrists and there was no way anyone could get out of them, without a key. And even if you had a key you would not be able to twist your fingers back far enough to get said key in the key hole and turn it.

He could not do it.

But with powerful binoculars trained on his hands, and without blinking, right there, right before my eyes, he wriggled his fingers and twisted his hands and he was free.

"That's impossible," I said louder than a whisper.

"Shhhh," said someone next to me. "You saw it. Nothing is impossible."

After the show I told those clogging up the back of the stage that I was a reporter and they led me right to Houdini's room. He loved publicity. That is why he picked the World Tower to hang from, so that the reporters would be right there looking out the windows.

He was rubbing his wrists when he welcomed me in.

And right there in front of me was the most plainspoken and underwhelming man imaginable.

"Hello," he said. "Have a seat and I will tell you everything you want to know."

He continued without me asking a question. "Was it a trick? Well, yes and no. Did I get outside help? No. Did I have a key? No. Do I have a secret? Yes. Will I share it with you? Yes."

So much would happen over the next ten minutes I could not take notes fast enough:

He was born in Hungary, the son of a rabbi. Moved to the US and changed his name from Erik Weisz because of anti-Jewish prejudice. Lived in abject poverty. Tried to be a magician but was not quick enough with his hands to fool anyone. Taught himself to escape from handcuffs. People did not believe it. Impossible, they said. Escaped from a straitjacket. People did not believe it. Impossible, they said. Escaped from underwater in chains. People did not believe it. Totally impossible, they said.

"But they still came out to see me do it and I was no longer poor," he told me.

As for tricks?

"Did you watch me when they put on the jacket?"

"Yes," I said.

"No, you didn't," he said. "I took many quick deep breaths. That made my chest bigger. When they tightened the straps I let out the air."

"That couldn't have given you much room," I said.

"Just enough to wiggle my shoulders and dislocate them."

"You what?!"

Pain shot through my lower stomach. The memory made me flinch. I had once dislocated a shoulder and it was excruciating.

"Then I could wiggle my hands around to the straps and unbuckle them."

"You what?!" I repeated.

"Impossible, they said. Ha."

I asked about the handcuffs.

"No tricks. No keys. I showed them at Scotland Yard. They locked up my hands. Impossible to get out of, they said."

He held his hands up in front of my face. "They can do impossible things."

He wove his fingers together the same as anyone could do, but then he bent one of his fingers back almost to his wrist. I felt that pain again.

"Their handcuffs had a way out, if you just put your fingers in places where your fingers could not go."

I was squeezing mine into a fist and putting them between my legs. That was too much pain.

"It's not impossible. And it's good that you know and write about it because those who see it don't believe it," he said. "They think it's a trick. But the trick is nothing is impossible."

And that is where I thanked him and said good night.

All my life I had heard nothing is impossible. But those were just words meaning "keep trying." But now I saw that something impossible was possible. Forget about how much pain you had to put yourself through, it was possible. Just knowing he got out of the handcuffs and straitjacket has gotten me though many problems. Nothing is impossible.

For those who did not believe he did things without a trick, he later devised the underwater escapes. He would be chained up and put into a large box, then it was filled with water and sealed up.

Three minutes later he would come up to the surface of the water. That is impossible. He kept himself in great shape. He could hold his breath for three and a half minutes.

But still, he was underwater. Chained. Sealed up. He could not breathe and there he was. Impossible, but there he was.

If he could do that I could handle a bad boss or a car that would not start.

Sadly, avoiding evil people is not possible. Three years after Houdini left Vancouver he was in Montreal to give a show. He had been on tour and broke his ankle in an earlier show.

He was resting on a couch in his dressing room when some students from McGill University came to visit. They had heard that Houdini said his stomach muscles were strong enough to withstand punches.

One of the students, a large football kind of fellow, without warning punched Houdini in the stomach with all his might.

Houdini had no chance to tighten his muscles. Then the student punched him again saying something along the lines of "You are supposed to be so strong."

And he punched him again. It ruptured Houdini's appendix.

He went on to performing the show, despite the pain in his stomach and his ankle. Then he continued on his tour, but in great pain.

Days later, on Halloween, he died.

Now here is one thing he thought was possible, and I know is possible, but he has not yet proved it. He told his wife Bess, who he met in his early years of performing, that after he died he would come back to her on another Halloween.

He never did. I will have to speak to him about what is possible.

THE WORLD

Speaking of murders—okay, they happen, even in nice books and in nice lives—there was once *Murder Most Foul*.

That was one of my favourite headlines in my early days as a reporter. I was working for the *Daily World*. You probably know the building at Cambie and Pender, the tall one with the naked ladies surrounding it, the one Houdini hung from. That was my first newspaper.

You probably get most of your news from television, which is good, but it's not a very active way of learning. You sit there and let someone tell you things.

Reading is better. That makes you part of the process—and you are part of it, aren't you? And you don't get sideswiped by commercials dancing, yelling, demanding and selling after you have been told the world may be ending.

It was the late 1800s and at the *World* the stories were as outrageous as they could make them.

Titanic Sinks. No One Hurt.

Some newspapers in supermarket checkout lanes are still like that, also some television stations. And the more out of whack with reality the stories are, the larger the audiences.

It is strange, but some of us like being lied to, and then we accuse others

Here are some of my colleagues from the *Daily World*. We rushed all over this city and were some of the first and most avid users of bicycles.

Harbour Publishing Archives

who don't agree with us of telling lies. As much as we may hate to believe it, people like being told things that are beyond belief, because look, it's on TV and in the paper or said by someone important.

And that makes those stories sell more than ordinary, fact-checked news.

When I was at the *World* there were five other reporters, all men. All wore suits and derbies, all rode bicycles and all roamed the city looking for big stories.

The best ones came from the waterfront. On June 2, 1890, a ferry boat pulled up to the wharf at Heatley Avenue and a few of the *World*'s scribes were waiting.

"You would not believe what I saw in Seattle," the captain shouted to the reporters even before the ropes were tied. "It was last night and I saw a man jump off a fishing boat docked near where we were tied up. He jumped into the water, which was strange since they were tied to the pier."

The reporters were already taking notes. They knew the source of the story: Captain John O'Brian. He was an old hand on the Seattle to Vancouver route.

"The water was shallow and he swam and pulled himself to shore then ran off into the darkness" the captain told them.

"Then what happened?"

"I saw some other men carry a fellow off the boat, down the wharf, across the street and into a saloon. So I followed them."

This is the sort of thing reporters love. An actual eyewitness telling first-hand what his eyes have witnessed.

"They laid him on a couple of barrels, then they ordered beer for themselves."

The reporters scribbled in their notebooks.

"I put my hands on the poor fellow and turned him over. He had been stabbed several times. There was no life in him. 'He's dead.' I said.

'Argument over money,' they told me. Then they went back to drinking, and I had to go back to my boat."

"Quite a story," said one of the reporters.

They rushed back to the newsroom and began work. With their pens dipped in ink they wrote about the dark, the fight, the yelling, the greed, the long history of animosity followed by the short changing of profits and finally the stabbing.

And then the vivid, better-than-television account of the body on beer barrels and the pronouncement of DOA, dead on arrival, by none other than a man from Vancouver.

And the headline: *Murder Most Foul.*

It did not matter that it happened in Seattle and there were no names of the victim or perpetrator or police statements. There was a name of the witness and that was enough.

The printers in the newsroom read the scribbled stories and took individual letters out of large drawers in a cabinet to spell out the words. It was the same as Gutenberg invented it four hundred years earlier, except now the letters were metal instead of wood.

The letters were all backwards, which makes printers the smartest people. And they were selected one by one. It was bad when they ran out of a letter.

"Hey, anyone have an 'S'"?

And the letters were arranged so the small ones were in the lower cases and the capitals were in the upper cases.

In case you ever hear anyone referring to capital letters as "upper case" or the regular letters as "lower case," there you go. If you have never heard of that tell your friends to learn a thing or two.

And then the letters were put in metal frames the size of a sheet of paper. When the frames were filled with the letters that became words—which became sentences, which became paragraphs, which became stories—the letters were covered with ink, using a roller that was covered with ink.

And then—I hope you are not bored because this changed the world—a sheet of paper was placed on the inked letters and a cover put on that and it was pressed down with a handle or wheel that gave it pressure. Do that a thousand times.

But, you caught that phrase, "pressed down." Hence the entire industry was called "the press."

L.D. Taylor
crook, newspaperman, politician
Cigar smoker
taylor in Chicago 1996 charged with embezzlement + Bigamy

You have to admit that was pretty interesting. The only thing that ruined that beautiful name was television. Now it is "the Media." No romance.

But *Murder Most Foul* was a work of poetic journalism. And it sold well, as all extreme stories do. The *World* made a fortune from stories like that.

During its heyday the *World* was owned by L.D. Taylor who was a character.

Here are a few notes I made about him...

DECISION

Prison

train ride

One Ticket as Far as I can go

VANCOUVER

Where's that?

HE worked For the Province Newspaper selling advertising

HE Bought The WORLD Newspaper

murder most Foul

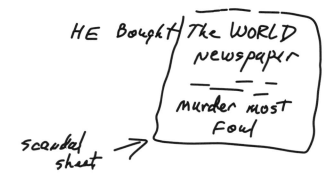

scandal sheet →

I'm a Newsman

House For sale

But he made his $$$ selling real estate ads

HE Built an
unusual shaped
Building For his paper

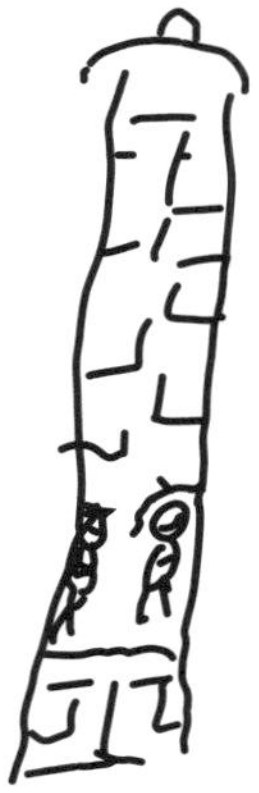

with statues of
Naked women
surrounding it.

Then real estate died
+ he lost his money

So he went into politics
+ was elected
mayor 8 Times

This is a
FUN City
NOT a
sunday school

But Then,

The police 
were corrupt

The mayor 
was corrupt

Gambling, prostitution
Drinking
OK!

women got The
vote

Men liked it

vote for
taylor

NO

women
Did not

But women could
Not vote

taylor lost
IN a land slide

+ spent The rest
oF his life
Bitter
+ died IN
poverty.

The END

THE FIRST PNE PRIZE HOME

The first PNE Prize Home, where Leonard and Emily spent a wonderful sixty years together.
Stuart Thomson photo, City of Vancouver Archives, AM281-S8-: CVA 180-0597

That last episode was not a good story, unless you want to sell a lot of newspapers and be a corrupt mayor, in which case it is good, which means that most stories are good and bad depending on where you hear them. That is a great lesson in life. Things you think are bad are bad, unless you hear them from the other side where they are good. Life can be difficult to understand.

But now here's one story that is all good, although it starts out bad.

I was covering the egg-laying contest at the PNE in 1934 when I saw a fellow who looked so sad.

We talked. His name was Leonard. He had no trouble telling me what was wrong with his life.

Leonard was in love with

Emily

HE WANTED to take her to The PNE

But EMily's FATHER

SAID NO!

LEONARD HAS No job No MoNey Not Even a car that works

Cough cough

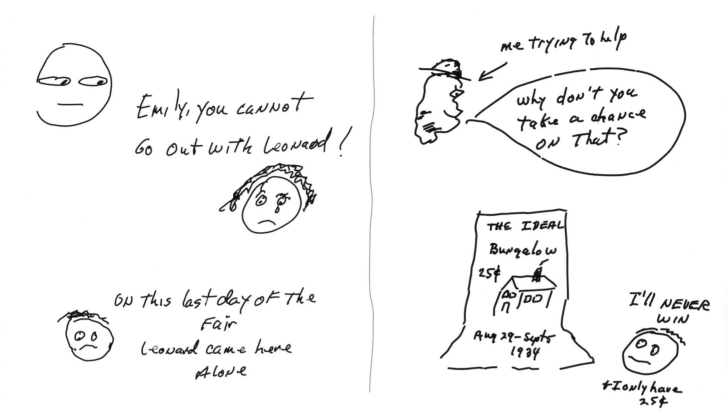

But in the end Leonard did take the gamble. We all should do that sometimes. He left the fair and walked home broke, tired, sad and hopeless.

Later that night while he was trying again to get the engine in his car to
start, which had not started for a month, he listened to the radio.

"And the first prize home winner is..."

There was a pause. "Leonard Frewin."

What?! How?! WHAT?! HOW?! WHAAAATTTTT!!!!!

HE RAN ACROSS TOWN TO EMILY'S HOUSE

Feet go Faster

But it was LATE

So he sat on the Front steps ALL NIGHT

EMILY'S FATHER SAID, OK

LEONARD Asked EMILY will you?

EMILY SAID, YES!

+ they Lived in the home

60 Years

and died within a month of each other.

THE END

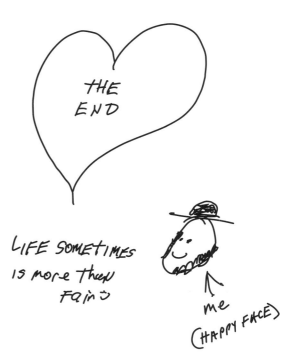

LIFE SOMETIMES is more then Fair

me (HAPPY FACE)

HAPPY FACES

One thing leads to another, always.

When I saw the happy face on me, last story, I remembered one of the world's great stories. Making something out of almost nothing.

When I met George Patey he had a big smile. How could you not like anyone who smiles?

He was an entrepreneur, which means someone who gets an idea and takes a chance on it. Sometimes that is good. Sometimes, well, you know. But at least they try.

For George it was an amazing story from gangster history. For me it was scary, because I was there.

His Name?

George.

He was what is called an Entrepreneur, which means He makes a living from Ideas & taks big risks

He had a bar in Gastown called Banjo Palace

Big exciting - Job not taught in school

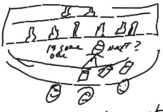

And it was doing ok - just ok

Then he read an article

in a newspaper (see, reading is good)

That said:

The warehouse where The St. Valentine's Day Massacre happened was being DEMOLISHED.

This was The place sacred - The Evil Holy place if There is such a Thing in Gangland history. as AN Evil Holy Place

It was the place in chicago in 1929 where AL Capone, the King of  crooks NICKNAMED ScarFace

Ordered his men to dress as policemen

& kill-shoot-kill

members of another
gang. — they were taking
away some of his profits
in Illegal BOOZE -- see, one
bad thing leads to another.

When the pretend police entered the warehouse the other bad guys thought it was just another visit to get some pay-off money.

Boy, were they surprised when the bad policemen told the bad guys to line up against the wall. And more surprised when they started shooting. So was I. This is not the kind of surprise you want.

The dead bad guys were dead and had their pictures in the newspapers. The pretend-police bad guys were never caught.

But the wall was still there, full of holes. It was a famous wall. And George bought it and in 1971 had it installed in the men's room of his new nightclub, with Plexiglas in front. Fun. For men.

"Bingo!" Or rather, "Can you believe I hit a hole in one?"

The wall was such a success that business in the bar was like a speak-easy before bars were legal.

But the wall was chicken feed in George's imagination. When I met him a few years later he was rich. He was having a party in the penthouse of his Beach Avenue condo. His partner, Bill Eliason, showed me around the

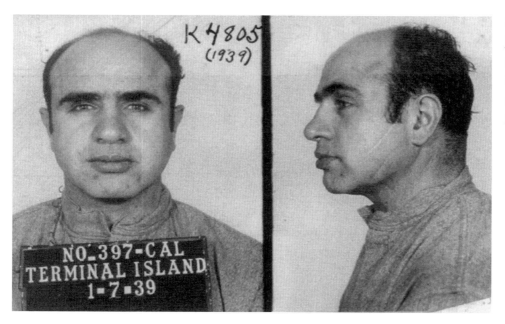

They did eventually jail the murderous gangster boss Al Capone, but only for tax evasion.

Photo courtesy www.fbi.gov

artwork, which was mostly floor-to-ceiling carvings from Indonesia so big you could slip behind them and disappear. That's big.

Then Bill said, would you like to see the whole apartment?

He started walking and where the condo should have ended it did not. We kept going into what would be the adjoining condo.

"We decided we would like a wrap-around view so we bought the place next to our place, and had the walls removed."

Rich, I thought.

George joined us. I had the idea he liked this conversation. It did not appear that it was the first time he had had it.

"You know where our money came from?"

"Holes in a wall"?

"Happy faces."

He said remember in the late 1960s and '70s, happy faces were everywhere? "So I had an idea."

Everyone was using rubber stamps with happy faces. He sold out before the smiles could fade. He made more stamps and sold out again. In short, he made a fortune, off a smile.

The happy face made George rich, and happy.

And the wall? He took it apart, gave some bricks away to friends and sold the rest.

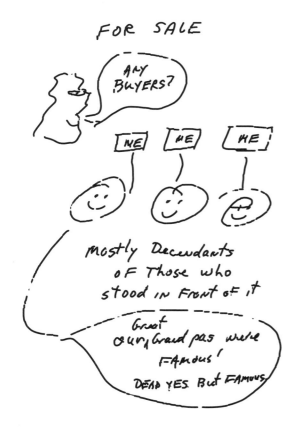

FOR SALE

ANY BUYERS?

NE   HE   HE

mostly Decendants
oF Those who
stood iN Front oF it

Great
our Grand pas were
FAMous!
DEAD YES But FAMOUS

But The Smile

The HAPPY FACE
MADE George Rich!

The moral:
DEATH by Bullet BAD
LIFE by smile Good

RUDOLPH

I went back to Chicago 10 years later — 1939

Becase someone told me a writer was having a problem

I writer

I like writers Especally ones who don'T have Deep Thoughts

Deep Thoughts

Not HAPPY

Bob was sad because his wife was sick. Worse than sick. She had cancer and he could not afford the medication. And he was caring for their young daughter.

It is hard to be cheerful when you are sad, but you must be or you will make someone else sad. Life is like that. It asks for a lot.

On top of that he had an assignment. Remember when you had a term paper due and you did not know what to write about and spelling counted?

Wait. Spelling does not count anymore. Kids now have spell check. As an old newspaper reporter I think that will bring down civilization.

Anyway, Bob had to write a story for Christmas for his company. They wanted to put out a colouring book and someone in head office said, "It should have a story, one of those Christmas type things."

And that went down to a lower office and a lower office and landed on the desk of Bob's boss.

"Bob, I want you write a Christmas story. The bigwigs want it. And make it snappy. And I don't have to tell you to make it good. My job depends on it."

Bob tried to raise his eyebrows but he could not. Behind them was a storm of pain, of: What? How? I can't! When? Why me?

"I don't care what you write about," said his boss. "Just make sure it's the best thing upstairs will read this season."

Then he added, "We are picking you because you've written some very fine underwear ads this year. I like that, 'Buy, buy, buy!' That's good writing."

I had just arrived in Chicago. When you are dead you can do a lot of travelling. Don't need a passport. I caught up with Bob when he was out with his daughter.

"My contacts tell me you had a tough childhood," I said.

Bob moved his head back a bit. I know he was thinking, "How do you know that?"

"Some of my hoodlum friends remember you getting beat up when you were a kid."

His eyes were opening and opening.

"And the other kids made fun of you because you were small."

If his eyelids got any wider his eyes would pop out.

"You're a lucky guy," I said. "You have some experiences to write about."

He and his daughter were at the zoo. She was looking at the reindeer. He saw me staring at her and the deer. "She likes them," he said.

I put my hands in my pockets and hunched forward like I imagined deep-thinking college professors would if they were trying to impress students.

"Your answer is in front of you," I said.

He still had a blank look.

"Look at the combination: bullied, and deer. Think about it. Creating something is just a matter of having something and creating with it and letting your mind go wild."

Bob went home that night and wrote about a reindeer that was bullied because of... what? His size? No. His name? No. What about his nose. Maybe he had an oddly coloured nose. Maybe that would work.

"All of the other reindeer used to laugh and call him names."

What Bob remembered was a terrible part of being ostracized: "They wouldn't let poor Rudolph join in any reindeer games."

But what he dreamed of that never came true was doing something that would make the other kids respect him: "Then one foggy Christmas Eve Santa came to say, Rudolph with your nose so bright won't you guide my sleigh tonight?"

What Bob wished for all his life: "Then how the reindeer loved him..."

And he added the crowning of something bigger than a wish: "...as they shouted out with glee, Rudolph the Red Nosed Reindeer you'll go down in history."

He did it. It took a little refining because writers always need that, and he was done.

His boss said, "I think this will do." He took it upstairs and they liked it and from there it went to a printer and a million colouring books had the story of Rudolph, and Bob got nothing. Not a raise, not a bonus, nothing, but he was allowed to stay at his low-paying job.

I thought of my sons and how they disappointed me and knew once

again life is not fair. Life is exciting, challenging, heartbreaking, beautiful, breathtaking, stomach turning, boring, and sometimes the best thing on earth, but it is not fair.

Get used to it. Sorry. That advice comes from someone who has more than several lifetimes of experience. Sometimes everything bad happens and you say, "Why?" The answer is just because it does.

If you can get over that you can survive anything.

Bob and I said goodbye and I went back to Vancouver.

Ten years later I got a letter from him. The company said Rudolph had run its course, it was old and flat and they no longer wanted it, so he could have it.

I was afraid he was going to say he put the story in a drawer under his socks and just wanted to thank me. But no. One of those most wonderful things happened—and all because he wanted it to happen.

His brother-in-law wrote songs and was pretty good at it. Bob asked him if there was anything he could do with Rudolph.

They cut down the words from a long story to a short song. The brother-in-law sent it to everyone famous but no one would record it.

However, as luck would have it—and luck simply plays a lot in life, don't ever stop wishing for it—the wife of Gene Autry saw it lying on her husband's desk. She read it and she liked it and you know what happens when a wife likes something.

Gene Autry was the singing cowboy who was super-famous back then. He recorded it and, hold your breath, it became the second most famous and most played Christmas song in history.

The first, because I know you are asking, is "I'm Dreaming Of A White Christmas." "Rudolph the Red-Nosed Reindeer" number two.

And finally Bob—and mostly his daughter who liked looking at the reindeer—got some good things out of an old assignment that had to be written quickly, and following his orders had "made it good."

I know you are saying this is not a BC story. On the other hand, of course it is. One: I met Bob and suggested how he could handle a problem and I am from Vancouver. Two: that suggestion applies to everyone everywhere. And most important, three: Rudolph flies over all of BC every Christmas.

But you know that. If you don't believe it just ask your kids.

MAJOR MATTHEWS

ajor James Skitt Matthews to be correct, although if you got the title and rank right you could forget about the other names. It was 1932 and I'd been sent to interview him because of his huge collection of Vancouver memorabilia.

The pictures were stacked up in a corner. No, wrong. They were stacked up in every corner from the floor to as high as you could put another picture on top.

Alongside the photos were papers, documents I guess, stacked just as high. And next to them were more papers, all neatly—wait a minute, what am I saying?—they were NOT neatly stacked. They were in piles and more piles. All papers.

And that was only on one side of one room. When I turned around there were more pictures and more papers, and then add hats on top of some piles.

Hats belonging to who? Don't know. But caps, and ladies hats, and army hats. Excuse me, Seaforth caps. Sitting on top of stacks of things.

"Hello. You want to interview me?"

It was Major Matthews, a large fellow standing in the space between the entrance room where I was and the dining room where he was, and behind him were stacks of papers and photos and, well look over there, dresses and coats on the backs of chairs.

"I would be delighted," I said. "I have heard you know everything about everything and a lot more."

Major Matthews straightened his large frame and like the horrific, pretentious officers I served under he said, "I do not have time for small talk. Get to the point or get out."

That was an interesting way to start an interview. Major Matthews was a bully. He had no kindness in his bulk. He was miserable.

But without him Vancouver would have no history. Period. You know all those pictures of Joe Fortes, the guy who did not own a restaurant but saved many lives and taught a generation how to swim? You know those pictures of him diving into the water? We would not have them if not for Major Matthews.

And how about that famous one of early Vancouver real estate sold on top of a giant stump on its side? Nope. You would never have seen it except for this miserable guy. And that ultra-important one of city hall after the great fire? You and we and no one would have seen that picture of the city's government in a tent if not for Major Matthews.

Let me add, he was also a nutcase, but then I never liked officers in the army. They commanded and we did the obeying. We died, they got medals.

James Skitt Matthews joined the Canadian army when World War I broke out. There is a minimal war record of his accomplishments, but we are sure he was a fine officer. He was promoted to major, which is the bottom of the top ranks.

First there is lieutenant, which means you are the officer who has to lead your troops into battle, and you often die. Then there is captain, which sounds great, but it only means you tell the lieutenants what to do. That

63

Major J.S. Matthews was a history enthusiast who appointed himself Vancouver archivist, long before Vancouver knew it needed one.

Steffens-Colmer Studios Ltd. photo, City of Vancouver Archives, AM54-S4-: Port P1713

is entirely different in the navy, where captains are in charge of battleships.

Sometimes an army captain would be assigned to a navy ship and suddenly he was treated like royalty. "Yes, I *would* like the roasted pheasant while you are chewing on the beef jerky. Thank you." And then he would go back to the army where he was told to pick up his K-rations.

That is a good education in the power and the triteness of a title. People living in the British Properties are high up, but even higher, although they have no views, are those living in Shaughnessy. Always be careful about name dropping, whether name, rank or address.

Back to Major Matthews. Major is one step above captain and it does not mean you are living in the British Properties or Shaughnessy, but maybe you are in the new Strathcona community, which was taken over from the former Black community and the Chinese community by white people remaking the hundred-year-old homes into a trendy and very nice middle ground between downtown's condos and the slums of East Hastings. Very, very good, but nothing to brag about.

Living in Strathcona is being a major: halfway up and respected and hard-working, but still closer to the enlisted than the elevated. And Major Matthews was fine with it.

Most, okay almost all, former army officers drop their rank and privilege after they take off their uniforms. Not Matthews. He insisted on being called "Major" for the rest of his life. If you can infer anything from that, congratulations to you. He liked status.

I was a sergeant. Sergeants do all the work that officers get credit for. After the wars and after the uniforms get put away then later get thrown in the recycling, sergeants don't, ever, use their rank. Enough said.

"What rank were you?" Major Matthews asked me.

I told him. He stared at me.

"Why am I talking to a sergeant?"

"Because you want your story told and after the war we are all equal and a sergeant, or even a cook, is now the same as a major." I wanted to go on but I also wanted the interview.

"A sergeant? Just a sergeant sent to interview me?"

This was getting to be fun. "Yup, sir."

And he wanted to tell his story.

"Follow me, sergeant."

We went upstairs to the attic. We actually went up a goat trail in the middle of the stairs. Every step had papers and photos and stuff, just stuff, piled to the next step.

We passed his wife in a sewing room on the second floor. "Would you tell him to clean up this stuff? He won't listen to me," she said in a voice that was not totally sarcastic.

The attic had little space left for us. We squeezed single file into the centre of the room where the major had a hard-backed chair and a table, with several piles of photos. (To give you an idea of the quantity, when his photos were later counted the number was half a million.)

I began my interview. "Okay, I'll make this simple. Why, how, and do you have any idea what is here?"

"The last question first: I know where everything is. When you love something you don't forget it and you don't lose it.

"Now the first question: because if I don't do this there will be no history of this city. None. The stupid—no that is not strong enough, the totally stupid—mindless and inept mayor and his minions don't give a rat's ass about the story of Vancouver. They want me to do all the work and they want to take the credit."

What had happened was the major had asked the mayor to store his stuff in city hall, which was agreed to, and all of the major's piles of stuff that he had stored at home and around town in every spare spot, in every friend's home or garage and every place he could rent, was moved to city hall.

But then the mayor said to the major that since we are supplying the storeroom then we are the owners.

"WHAT?!" said the major. "You are out of your mind!"

"However," the mayor added to soothe the major, who had not yet fully exploded, "we will give you the title of the city's unofficial archivist."

"What??!! You will WHAT, you will WHO?!!?" Major Matthews said.

Matthews said other things too, but this is a family tour of the history of the province. "Unofficial archivist," said the major, to whom titles were gold. "UNOFFICIAL?"

The mayor said yes.

So the major, along with some friends, moved everything out of city hall and into his home at 1158 Arbutus Street in Kitsilano.

To bring this to an end, the city did eventually give in and allowed the major to move his stuff to the castle over the Burrard Street Bridge. That was one heck of a job. Stopping halfway across the bridge then carrying the boxes up and stacking them and going back for more. But Major Matthews was happy.

Before I go on, you know that pretend castle, right? Over the Burrard Bridge. Pretend you know. Good. I knew you did. It was built just to hide the ugly steel superstructure that holds up the bridge, and you knew that.

His treasures sat there comfortably, until pigeons and rain got in.

And while he was still alive, which is the best time to do things, Major Matthews was in fact made the city's official archivist. And after he passed into the parade grounds in the sky the official city archives was built underground in Vanier Park, where his stuff will be safe forever. And it was named the Major Matthews Building. It was the first official archives in Canada.

And if it was not for him, the building with all those incredible photos and documents would be empty. In fact, there would be no building. Those pieces of real history would be scattered in scrapbooks and basements around the city, probably forgotten, possibly destroyed, and unknown.

In the end, I salute you Major Matthews.

ANOTHer Good lesson

You don't
have to be
sweet +
Nice

to do good
Things.

Consider
who you
criticize.

That person
might be
SAVING The
world.

SISTER FRANCES

I've got to tell you about Fanny. When it comes to loving, sacrificial, caring and conniving there was none better.

Fanny was Sister Frances, who was a deaconess of the Church of England. Or she was not. She was a certified midwife and nurse. Or she was not. She was a recipient of the Victoria Cross. Or not.

Fanny did more good in one life than basically anyone else I know, and that is fact.

I met her when she was taking a stagecoach to Lytton in 1888. She was sitting on some luggage, which was hard on her bottom and had no support for her back.

"Were you really in the Boer War, and got wounded and got the VC?" I asked.

"So they say," she said. No smile. No trying to be coy. But I knew there had been no Victoria Crosses awarded to women as of then.

The coach rocked terribly and she bounced up and came down hard and said nothing.

"Why Lytton?"

"Because people need care and there are no nurses there." This time she smiled. We were now talking in the area she liked.

I knew she was from England, or Northern Ireland, take your pick. And I knew that after the time she went to nurse the troops in the bottom of Africa, she married and came to Canada, to Winnipeg. She was there only one year, 1887, before she and her husband, in the polite way of putting it, went their separate ways.

And that is when Fanny went her way: straight to Montreal, where she enrolled in the nursing school at the University of Laval, which yes, was then in that city. The only problem was Laval did not admit women in the nineteenth century.

There was a school of midwifery at another campus that would later become the University of Montreal and there is a line in their books of her being "examined" there, but no record of what happened.

And, because she never slowed down, she took courses to be a deaconess of the Anglican Church. However courses did not begin in Canada until five years later.

Sister Frances cared for the sick, taught nurses, and opened a hospital.
City of Vancouver Archives, AM54-S4-: Port P128.1

Still, a little later that same year, 1887, a friend of hers was contacted by a friend in Vancouver who was looking for nurses. Well, *she* was a nurse, and a midwife, and a deacon of the church. She was Sister Frances, a title she apparently gave herself, and she was off to Vancouver.

The friend in Vancouver was the rector of St. James Church, just a few steps away from the Hastings Mill. It was, like now, and sad how that happens, an area of poverty, unemployment and alcoholism.

Only back then add unspeakable injuries from the cruel world of giant logs and spinning saws. And now add unspeakable injuries from the cruel world of drugs and crime.

But we want to talk of good things. Sister Frances helped open a hospital,

69

one of the city's first, across the street from the Powell Street Grounds, which would later become Oppenheimer Park. And she started a nursing school. The first class had one student.

"How and why?" I asked. "You did so much. Again, how and why?"

"It is what a nurse does," she said.

"You're now going into a place with typhoid and smallpox. Aren't you afraid?"

"It is what a sister of the church does," she said.

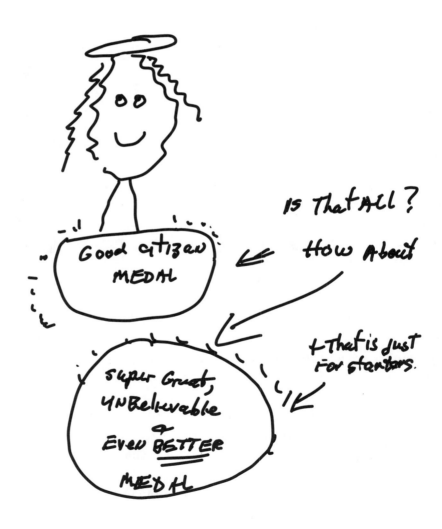

"Fanny—" I started to say and then she cut me off.

"Only you can call me Fanny."

Sometimes you fall in love with a person just from a few words, and a lot of action.

The hospital, which opened with seven beds, grew and Sister Frances gave free care to those who could not afford to pay. And she took in orphans—kids who were brought to the hospital because of illness but had no place to go after they were cured. She raised two boys and officially adopted one girl.

Just over thirty years after she started caring for those in pain she received an actual award that she could hang around her neck. In a large ceremony on June 13, 1929, in front of the bandstand on Beach Avenue at English Bay, she was awarded the Good Citizenship Medal.

She got something else that year, which you can still see. Six blocks of Keefer Street, from Vernon to Victoria, were renamed Frances Street.

It ends just at the Bosa food store on Victoria. You can get a good Italian sandwich there and eat it while walking down Frances Street and think of what just one person can do. In the sandwich are defiant hot peppers, soothing provolone cheese, and sustaining salami.

The Victoria Cross? It is hard to say to all those who received it, but she did as well as them, maybe better.

CYCLING

I would like to talk to you about the history of transportation here. It is not the SkyTrain or buses. Just think of *zip*, maybe *zoom*, or other words that mean terrible speed coming out of nowhere and missing you or me by very little.

I was on Georgia Street, walking.

"Oh, come on. Do you have to ride your bike on the sidewalk?"

That's me shouting at the rider of a bike way down the end of this sidewalk before he went through a red light and up onto another walkway.

"In the old days you would have been fined!"

He did not hear me.

But in the old days, anyone riding on the sidewalk would have gotten a five-dollar penalty, and that was a day's pay. We didn't fool around back then.

Of course the constable would have to catch said bicycle law breaker and there is no chance of that.

Bikes flew by fast then, like now. And the safety bikes were on the sidewalks. You know the safety bikes, don't you? The ones like you ride now? Oh, I have so much to tell you.

Go back to the 1880s. No cars. Lots of horses and some trains that ran

During their first heyday in the 1880s, bicycles revolutionized commuting in Vancouver.

W.M. Bruce photo, City of Vancouver Archives, AM1592-1-S2-F05-: 2011-092.0289

on tracks in the middle of the street, and were colourful and fun, but they were only going that way when of course you wanted to go the other way where there were no tracks.

And then came this wonderful invention. The bicycle, you know the ones with the giant wheel in front and the tiny thing in the back. You call them penny-farthings, but we didn't. That name came in just as they went out of fashion and were picked up by collectors. Collectors need names for what they collect and penny-farthing was the name. We just called them bicycles.

And there was no fear of the ones with the giant wheels riding on the sidewalk. They could not get over the curb. And if they did there was not enough room to wiggle, which they did.

They were the hot rods of early speed. The young men who got them, and they were always young men because women in their skirts could not get up there and older men could not stay up, loved them.

Getting on was a breathtaking moment of crossed fingers. Except you didn't cross your fingers. You grabbed the handlebar, which you could barely reach, and put one foot on a peg above the back wheel. Then you pushed forward to gain speed and quickly jumped onto the seat while trying to steer and keep your balance.

I tried once and the bike started tipping over and I looked down and there was a long way to go and by the time I got to the end of that long way and slammed into the street I said NEVER would I go up there again.

But others did and for about ten years high wheels, that's also what we called them, were everywhere. And could they go fast. With each revolution of the pedals almost fifteen feet of wheel passed over the ground. That was low-level flying.

Unless you hit something. With the wheel sometimes as high as five feet up, if it suddenly stopped you would fly over the handlebars and end up with a bloody mess at the best of times.

Sometimes you would die, and that was a bad way to end a bicycle trip. If someone had invented bicycle helmets back then we might all still be riding high wheels.

It got so scary that if you were going downhill you would put your feet up over the handlebars so that if you did hit a rock or horseshoe your legs would go over first while the rest of you followed.

And even if you did not get maimed there was still the problem of getting back up.

Hence, you can see why bikes with two even, normal-sized wheels were called safety bicycles. It took no time flat to see the high wheels disappear after the low wheels appeared in the late 1880s.

And everyone who could afford them had them. No horse to feed. No shoes to scuff. And no excuse that you missed the streetcar and could not get to work on time.

This was great. We had the wind in our faces and exercise under our feet. Nothing could be better. Bicycle paths were everywhere, all made of crushed stone and cinder. But still *zoom, zip,* some idiots still rode on the sidewalks, which were smoother.

"Hey, ride in the street!"

The things that finally got the bikes off the sidewalks were cars. When they came in the early 1900s everyone wanted one, even if they couldn't afford it.

Who wants to pedal and get sweaty and face cold winds? For almost a century, except for children, bicycles disappeared.

And now the rebellion against cars is getting people back on bikes, and riding on the sidewalk to avoid the cars. Who wants to use a bike path? They don't go where I want to go.

But bikers do have a problem: "Those idiots on motorized skateboards are a menace."

And I say to them: "Try something old-fashioned. Take a hike." It worked for me. Slow, gentle, healthy, reliable, fashionable. Just keep your eyes open, especially on the sidewalk.

TORCHY

His hair was on fire. Flames shooting out behind his head. A fire in a windstorm.

When Torchy ripped past you it was worth the forty cents you spent for your seat, even though forty cents would buy you a first-class dinner with steak.

In the mornings kids could get in for fifteen cents, and that would give them bragging rights right through elementary school.

But for you, you could say, "I saw Torchy last night. He's the fastest man on earth without a motor, you know." And whoever was listening, wishing they had been there, knew that.

William "Torchy" Peden rode a bicycle with no gears and no brakes. He rode it around and around with no scenery, no switchback hairpin turns, no hills except the sloping side of the track and basically no rules, except go faster than you are now going, and then go faster.

And when the pain is unbearable, go faster.

The races lasted six days and six nights. They were held in the Denman Arena, that great sports and culture palace at Denman and Georgia. Shame you don't have it anymore. It was cozy and warm, not like—well never mind not like what. Pity you don't have it. Burned down in the 1950s.

But in the 1930s, when few had jobs and entertainment was desperately needed, there were the six-day bike races.

The riders kept going no matter what on bikes with curved handlebars and pedals and nothing else. No brakes, no gears, no coasting, no water bottles. Oh sure, you could stop for a drink and food, but then you would be behind.

They did not have the luxury of the Tour de France where you actually get to sleep at night and start out in the morning after breakfast. Those are wimps compared to the six-day riders.

This was more like the Roman chariot races that ended when most of the horses and drivers were mangled or killed, and that was usually in time for lunch.

The six-day races were made better when the sport introduced two-man teams. Then they could keep going if someone had to stop because the top of his head was sheared off, which happened in a race I was watching. Poor fellow ploughed into a concrete and steel wall, not good to have those on a course for a bike race, and took off much of his top. He got thirty-eight stiches and his partner had to keep riding for eleven hours waiting for him.

Now that's a sport.

But Torchy survived most of the races unharmed because he was usually in front. The crashes happened behind him.

In 1929 he was once clocked officially at eighty-one miles per hour. That's 130 kms. It did not last for long, but he did it. No one else ever did.

And again, this was on a bike with fat tires and no gears. All just legs.

In his first four years as a professional six-day racer he won twenty-four of forty-eight races. Nobody did that now or then. In fact, nobody did that,

SOME ONE'S SCARF

81 mph (130km)

NO ONE CAN GO THAT FAST! IMPOSSIBLE! BAT NOTHING IS

except Torchy. And because of that he made a lot of money. Bless him. Anyone who does things no one else can has earned it.

During the Depression he was the second highest paid athlete in the world after Babe Ruth, who did it mostly standing still and swinging a piece of wood.

By the way, Babe Ruth was once in Vancouver. I'll tell you about it later.

The thing about Torchy was, he was nice. So was the Babe. That proves something important. Hero worship sometimes can be a good teacher.

Oh, one other thing. I mentioned earlier the Tour de France: riders have water bottles, and the winners have fame and there is occasionally corruption, which makes it interesting. But as much as they look like they are super-athletes, and they are, they ride about 2,200 miles in twenty-one days.

In the single-man contests of the early six-day races, a single rider rode 2,088 miles (forget about the metric conversions, just look at the numbers) in SIX DAYS.

Then came three speeds and ten speeds and custom lightweight racing bikes and mountain bikes and Torchy was out of work, but still rich.

That was a good ending to a good life and what more can you wish.

JOHN SULLIVAN DEAS

More transportation news. You are driving south on Highway 99. You go into the George Massey Tunnel, or bridge or flotation device or whatever they decide, if they ever do decide on anything, and STOP.

No, don't stop. Of course not. Don't listen to what people tell you, even if the person is a ghost and knows things others do not.

But stop in your mind. George Massey was a fine fellow. He was a politician. His real name was Nehemiah Massey, but people called him George. It was his work that brought you the tunnel that replaced the picturesque but plodding Ladner ferry.

But the name for the underwater passage that he and others wanted and got was the Deas Island Tunnel. That is the name Queen Elizabeth commemorated when she opened it in 1959. Eight years later, after George Massey died, the name changed.

I met John Sullivan Deas in his cannery right above where the tunnel is now.

He looked so pleasant, like the fellow you wished would be your neighbour. How could anyone put a man like him in chains and say he was their property? (Of course, how could you say that about anyone, no matter what

80

they looked like? It was just that how could you do something so bad to someone who looked so good?)

But John Sullivan Deas was a slave for the first twenty-five years of his life. He lived and worked on a plantation in South Carolina. He did what he was told to do. He served—in truth, he slaved—for someone else with nothing in return and no hope things would ever change.

He was born a slave and he would die a slave.

Then came Abraham Lincoln, and although people now say he was not as broadminded as his reputation he did write and issue the Emancipation Proclamation and John Sullivan Deas was a free man.

Lincoln later paid for that with a bullet through the back of his head.

As soon as Deas was set free, he and his wife Fanny headed for a place he had heard about from others who heard about it. The gold fields out west. He would now be his own master, what a beautiful thought. It was hard work, but nothing is as hard as working and getting nothing in return, and that was all he knew.

When he got to where the gold was in 1864, which was Yale, British Columbia, he basically had to push through the crowds of miners and prostitutes and saloon keepers and thieves to get to the river where there might be gold.

But there was no gold. He told me whatever had been there was gone. But he could do something else.

Deas was a special slave. He was too valuable to spend all day every day picking cotton. He was taught to make things out of tin. Tinsmithing was a necessary craft before factories made and dollar stores sold everything,

Someone had to make the dinner plates and cups and coffee pots and candle holders and smaller farm tools and that was the tinsmith. It took years to master, but he actually had a skill, a rarity for Black slaves. He fashioned pots and pans and kettles and tools. He hammered thin iron sheets and cut them into usable items and soldered them and coated them with a variety of other metals dug from the ground.

It was all a modern miracle. The coatings kept the iron from rusting.

And in Yale, where there was no gold for him, he turned back to tin. He started making the things people needed for living, while hoping more gold would be found. He was the town tinker. The only problem was, which he did not know, that tinkers did not live very long. But no one ever admits there is a problem with what they are doing if what they are doing is giving them a living, and a good one. And there was a way he could make a much better one.

Deas was told the real gold in this new land was salmon. They were in endless supply only a hundred miles to the south and the way to get rich from them was to put them in cans that would not rust. And he knew how to make cans that would not rust.

And just at the spot where you enter the Massey Tunnel under the Fraser River he built a cannery. There was no problem getting salmon. It was the cans that were needed.

In short time he taught others his craft and he made some simple machines that would stamp out thousands of sheets of iron and then coat them with chemicals and other metals.

Ex-slave John Sullivan Deas created a booming cannery village on the Fraser River and gave his name to Deas Island.

Image D-05348 courtesy of the Royal BC Museum and Archives

He hired scores of Indigenous people and Chinese labourers and drifters to cut and pack the fish, which he bought from everyone who would bring them to him.

He was a master who paid his people.

John Deas opened the first cannery on the lower Fraser River. Even when competition came he was the number-one canner on the river, with his own label that was well known in England, where most of his fish went.

And the cannery is where I met him.

"I don't want to talk about those bad times," he said when I asked him about slavery.

But working with the tin was killing him. No energy. Hard breathing.

Other things went into making the tin to keep the metal from rusting, bad things. Two were mercury and lead. Bad. But the worst was asbestos.

It is harmless if it is not disturbed. Once it was on the tin it hurt no one. But getting it there was a toxic process. And it was sneaky. Those working with it had no idea they were breathing in microscopic slivers of chemical knives that were slicing apart their lungs.

And now he and his wife had seven children and were doing well. But after his one cannery there soon were a dozen, then two dozen, and more were coming.

Deas sold his company in 1878. Two years later he died. He was forty-two.

The tunnel was renamed for George Massey, a politician who had it built.

But as for Deas, well, there is a park nearby—the Deas Island Regional Park—and it is free for all people.

TREE HOUSE

Yes, I know you have a housing problem. Well, so did we. In 1900 two years' pay was needed for a small lot on Victoria Drive, when it was still bush and tall blackened half-burned stumps were the neighbourhood public art.

And then you build a shack on it and a year later prices have gone up and some developer says, "We would like to build a large Victorian home on your land for one of the managers of the mill down the street."

You say no and then he adds, "Three years' pay right on the barrel head, this minute."

And you look at the barrel and all that money and say, "What an opportunity. Sold!"

That is what a fellow named Berkman said. He took the money and then discovered three years' pay would now get him only a lot in Burnaby and he was not sure where Burnaby was.

So he went deep in the logged forest looking for a place to call his own. That's where I met him while I was hunting for mushrooms. Ponderosas, so good fried with butter and nothing else.

We exchanged greetings and he asked if I would help him search for that special place.

Helping is good, also the mushrooms were hard to find. Since most of the trees had been cut the mushrooms were vanishing. They grow just at the base of both hemlocks and cedars, but not when the trees are not there. We did not call it global warming, but we said it was sad.

The forest was now a moonscape of stumps. Some were towering, a few just tall, all of them burned—the most efficient way of getting rid of them. And the smoke from the burning hung over the whole of everything. In truth, in what was supposed to be the forest there was no fresh air.

However, after a few minutes of walking Berkman said, "Look over there. Right there."

And at that spot were the stumps of two cedars that had grown together. They were tall and massive around. If you measured them both with one rope it would be almost sixty feet. That would make what would later be called a mega house.

The fabled stump house at Twenty-sixth Avenue and Seacombe Road in Vancouver looked like something out of a fairy tale.

W.J. Moore photo, City of Vancouver Archives, AM54-S4-: SGN 988

One of the stumps was only about six feet high, but the other was more than twice that, still small compared to the ones around it that were burned, but tall enough for Berkman.

"Perfect," he said.

"For what?"

"For living in. And no one owns it and no one wants it," he said.

Technically he was wrong. They were all owned by the logging company, which was a subsidiary of the mill, which was owned by a conglomerate of wealthy men who lived in the mansions along Blue Blood Alley. That would be West Georgia to you.

"They," he told me, "have no idea where this is and they won't care." And this would be his home.

He said he would tell his wife the good news. He went to town and brought her back. I waited and thought of my home on the north shore. It had a view. It had running water from a creek. This had, if you added imagination and faith in yourself, something real estate agents always say: it had potential.

"Are you out of your mind?" said his wife.

I know this because I was there, because the theatre is not the only place to watch comedy and drama. Besides, Berkman asked me to stay because he might need some support.

"And who is this old-looking fellow with you?" she asked.

"Just a friend I met in the woods. He knows his way around."

"You meet someone in the woods and now you want me to live in a stump? And I married you?"

He begged her to give him two weeks and then decide. Meanwhile she could take their three kids and move in with a friend of hers in a shack that measured ten feet by twelve feet.

Simply put, he had two weeks to save his marriage or spend a lifetime sleeping in the chicken coop.

Then Berkman asked if I could help. I never asked if Berkman was his first or family name. Major Matthews later wrote under a photo of the tree house that it belonged to "a Mr. Berkman," but no first name. He just referred to himself as Berkman and I accept what others say.

He got a couple of axes and saws and mallets and the two of us started cutting away. The front door of the shorter stump was easy, and once inside the trunk was mostly hollow. That was why the loggers cut above it. We cleaned out that trunk and it would be the kitchen. If he was alive now he would have his own TV reality show on making something out of nothing.

Then we cut through the inside wall that joined the two stumps and in the taller trunk hollowed out another space. Presto, the living room. And no door between the kitchen and living room, giving it that open concept, which is now in demand on the reality shows. "I can watch the children while working in the kitchen," the wife always says, while she is really thinking, "Can't I get away from them anywhere?"

And over the living room we put in a ceiling. Then we used a ladder outside to get through another opening in the trunk and cleaned out the makings of a bedroom on the second floor. Not much privacy, but it was sturdy.

Add a door and a few windows, along with a roof for each wing, and his wife said, "What will my friends say?"

"They will hire us to make homes like this for them," Berkman said. "It will be a new style, a new way of living. It has two more rooms than our old shack. Plus through ecological, natural insulation it will be warm in winter and cool in summer."

In truth, he crossed his fingers and said, "It's bigger than the shack."

"Oh, now I love it," she said in his dreams. But she stayed and had two more babies.

They were there five years before the logging company came. "You need to go," they said. "We are clearing this area to put in houses."

Later this place would be known as 4230 Prince Edward Street. That is Prince Edward between Twenty-sixth and Twenty-seventh Avenues. But then it was just that spot over there.

No deed. No equity. They went back to Victoria Drive to see a row of large homes that were not there before they left. I heard they moved to Burnaby, and built a small, comfortable home. "This one at least we own," he said.

I lost contact with Berkman but I did hear from someone who heard from someone that their home was near what would become Willingdon and Lougheed. Hope it was true, although their descendants would have to put up with the noise of the SkyTrain and the construction of the condos and those annoying offers of a million dollars for their home. Cash. Right on the barrel head.

SMOKEY SMITH

I loved Smokey. It was not because he was probably the bravest or craziest soldier I have ever known, but because he was a rotten soldier who I would have put in the stockade and then later told all my recruits to be like him, only don't be.

Besides Smokey, I love the contradictions of life. They are the spices that give it a flavour that makes you say, "Wow, I like that."

Okay, enough mindless confusion.

Smokey Smith, as you know—and you had better know or I will personally stare you down until you say, "Please, tell me what I should know"—was the only private in World War II in the entire Canadian army, which included endless numbers of brave men, to get the Victoria Cross.

You get that for only one thing: mindless incredible unbelievable bravery in the face of the enemy.

That is what Smokey had and did. He also did one other thing. He did not do what others told him to do, and as a career soldier I said you had to obey orders. If you did not you would have a bunch of uniforms bumping into each other. They had to march in the same direction or there would be no army. Smokey said phooey.

You CANNOT have a soldier saying phooey. Sorry I raised my voice.

Except for Smokey.

Here is the story you know so I don't have to tell you.

It was raining. No, it was pouring and my hands were swollen from the water and I was miserable.

But I was lucky. I was behind the church in that small Italian town and I could see Smokey heading down the road with another private, Jim Tennant. They were by themselves on the other side of the river from me and the rest of their unit, who I was trying to help. There was some small arms fire and I saw Jim go down.

I knew Smokey wouldn't leave him. Of course not. He was a guy who lived with an exuberant, fearless code of his own that rejected rules and accepted doing what needed to be done.

Often that was having another beer after he should not have had another beer and after the pub was closed and after the army curfew.

He was a private. But he was a good private. He knew his weapons, he knew the strength of loyalty and comradeship and pride in being a Seaforth Highlander, but he also knew the army would not stop him from living as he wanted to live.

He was promoted to corporal nine times, and demoted nine times. Most of the times beer was part of what happened. But even without beer he would not do as he was told. Those are the soldiers who wind up confined to quarters, in the stockade and released with a less than honourable discharge.

Back to that night of October 21, 1944. Out of the darkness and rain I saw Smokey pick up Jim and carry him to a ditch alongside the road while the enemy was firing at them. He came back onto the road and open fire with his Tommy gun.

This was bare knuckles fighting with bullets.

Then I heard the rumble of the tank. I heard it but Smokey saw it and it was almost on top of him.

"Oh my god," I whispered. "He's going to die."

Ernest "Smokey" Smith was the only Canadian private to win the Victoria Cross in World War II.

Jack Lindsay photo, City of Vancouver Archives, AM1184-S3-: CVA 1184-803

It was a Panther, a medium-weight attack tank that killed with impunity. It was a dragon that had no fear. And it was ten yards away from him. Ten yards, thirty feet. Ten metres if you like. One down in football. It doesn't take many steps to go ten yards.

Smokey grabbed his anti-tank gun, which is the name for a weapon that fires one small rocket at a time. The rocket explodes if you hit something like a tank. It does nothing if you miss. And by the time you reload you would be dead.

And Smokey just stood there in the middle of the road aiming his anti-tank gun. The ground in front of him was being chewed up with fire from the tank.

How could they miss him? But they did long enough for Smokey to pull the trigger and *bam*, the tank was hit between a wheel and the tread, which blew off the endless wraparound foot that drove the dragon forward.

It stopped. And from around the protection of the rear of the tank came the soldiers. Smokey dropped his anti-tank weapon and grabbed his Tommy gun. One guy against ten and everyone is shooting.

I saw four of the enemy go down and the others retreat behind the tank. Then a second tank came. Smokey was fast. He grabbed the anti-tank gun that Jim had been carrying and ran straight at it.

One man with one hand-held weapon charging a massive moving piece of steel with a cannon sticking out of it. Crazy.

I was trying the stop the bleeding of one of our guys. I could not run out and help Smokey or the soldier at my feet would bleed to death and Smokey would still die. And even though I could not die again I was scared. Some feelings never die.

Smokey fired. The tank was hit and slid down a shallow ravine. More soldiers came out from the rear and Smokey grabbed his Tommy gun again and started firing. Until he ran out of ammunition.

Then he ran back to where Jim was. Smokey had been a runner in high school in New Westminster, a very fast runner, and that's how he got the nickname Smokey. He was more than ten years older now and wearing army boots covered with mud and carrying thirty pounds of weapons and he looked like he was on a school track.

He found some magazines that were left behind in a ditch and loaded his Tommy gun and fired again. He kept firing and reloading until all the magazines were empty.

Smokey picked up Jim and carried him closer to our side. By this time our guys had gotten across the river and Smokey joined them in attacking the incoming third tank, which was destroyed, along with two artillery pieces.

It happened so quickly.

The official account of it has more precise details of the movement of each tank and each enemy soldier and where Smokey was and what he was firing. But in truth, it all happened so quickly you could get a different version from each witness, just like a car accident on the street seen by three people with three totally different ways of saying how it happened.

In short, Smokey was a one-man army.

Smokey, who was officially Ernest Alvia Smith but was never, ever called that except once, was smiling. He had a soft smile that meant he knew everything he was doing but pretended innocence. It was a good trait for winning girls and talking yourself out of trouble.

"That's the bravest thing I have ever seen," I said to him.

"I didn't do anything. I was just trying to keep Jim alive."

I told him, "I know you do not like following orders, but your orders were to hold that position, and you did that."

"Don't be daft," he said. "I was holding the position because I had to, not because I was following orders."

Who could not love him after that?

And then he was awarded the Victoria Cross, the only private in World War II. The night before he was to fly to England for the presentation the army put him in jail, just to make sure he would be on the plane in the morning.

As Smokey told me, "I said what the hell is this, but then they gave me a couple of beers in my cell and I was happy."

And in front of King George VI Smokey was Smokey. He was told to bow, he must bow, he darned well better bow, but Smokey did not bow. However he did salute.

He would not follow orders. And that almost always gets you into trouble.

However, he did substitute for an entire army without being told to. And that got him out of trouble.

Two months before he died I was proud to be watching when he was presented with the Pukka Award. It was given by Sappers to someone who would then be an honorary Sapper.

Smokey cherished it. He said there were fewer Pukka Sappers than Victoria Cross winners.

And the best thing about the Victoria Cross, in Smokey's words? "I was given the VC and told to put it in my pocket. I wasn't allowed to wear it for at least three days so the Canadian newspapers would have the photo the same time as the British ones. So for three days, I'm sitting in a bar in London drinking to beat hell. Someone came in and said, 'Okay, Smokey, you can put on that medal now.' So I took it out and put it on my chest, and I never bought another drink that day."

It was a valuable medal.

MICKEY
O'ROURKE

You probably would not have liked him. I didn't either. I loved him, but didn't like him. I felt sorry for him but like you I might put his picture in a frame and hang it in a room of Canadian heroes. In fact, that is where it is.

But he was a drunk, and that is not good. I pulled him out of the gutter a couple of times and helped him get home. And home was a single room in a fleabag hotel on East Hastings.

He was an orphan from an early age and he worked in a coal mine.

Now if you left Mickey aside for a moment, and you met another fellow in this story, William Foster, it was probably at a cocktail party in Shaughnessy. Everyone liked him. He would be wearing his chestful of medals on his chief constable uniform. He would not have too much to drink and only nibble at the smoked salmon appetizers. His image was important.

He came from a good family and had an excellent education.

A fine man, who had the moral fibre of a bum, whereas Mickey had the fibre of a gentleman.

Let me take you back to a warm day in 1935. Longshoremen were striking. They had terrible pay and awful working conditions and they wanted to be treated better. When they walked off the job the shipping companies hired scabs to do the work at even less pay.

94

And on this day in June more than a thousand longshoremen gathered at the foot of Heatley Avenue, which led to the docks. They wanted to protest. And they wanted to look respectable. All of them wore suits and ties, which for most was their only suit and tie.

The shipping executives and the police said strikes were a sign of communism, and they would stop them. No talk, no negotiations, just stop them.

The longshoremen began marching toward the docks. In the lead was Mickey O'Rourke, who held the Union Jack up high. It hurt a great deal because he had sciatica problems brought on by his time in the war.

If you have ever had sciatica problems you know the pain is excruciating. It starts in your lower back and goes down one leg with such intensity it makes your leg crumple.

Mickey had that, and he kept marching.

William Foster saw the marchers from his vantage point several blocks away. He hated them. He hated everyone who was a threat to his upper-class style of living. There were two classes of people to him, his people at the top and those others at the bottom.

He ordered every constable to attend to the situation with their riot sticks, which were hickory filled with lead. They hurt. And he ordered all the armed police to the head of the line, and he had back-ups: a hundred Mounties on their horses, also with riot sticks.

As the men with ties and suit jackets marched forward the police attacked. It was not the other way around.

Clubs went swinging at heads and backs. Tear gas was shot at a tent where wives of the longshoremen were ready to treat the injured, just in case there would be any.

The battle went on for three hours. Three hours of beatings and blood and one, luckily only one, protester shot in the back of his legs. Yes, the back of his legs.

The protest failed, of course. And Mickey went back to his miserable life.

During the war he suffered what they then called shell shock, now post-traumatic stress disorder. He got that while he was saving others. You see, when he went to join the army he was told he was too old to join. He was thirty-nine. The army wanted young men who could fight.

95

He wanted to serve, but he did not want to kill anyone. He was given a stretcher and told he would rescue others. And that is what he did.

In many battles he ran into the fire of the enemy and picked up the wounded and carried them back to a trench on the safe side. Well, the safer side, at least for a while.

But one day facing heavy machine gun fire he saw a Canadian soldier stumbling blindly in no man's land. In full view of the enemy Mickey went over the top of the trench and ran to the rescue of the other man.

The dirt was flying in his face from the bullets hitting in front of him. Of course if one had hit him this would be a different story.

He ran totally without fear. Maybe he was crazy. You cannot tell what a person is thinking when facing death. Sometimes there is no thought. They are just facing death and you don't think about that.

For the next three days he went out over and over in the face of machine guns and poison gas to rescue downed men. He was buried once by the mud and dirt being kicked up by the bullets. That is a lot of bullets and a lot of dirt.

For three days and three nights he did not stop. He did not rest, he did not quit, he did not eat. He kept going out to save others in a war where he said he would do no harm.

No one knows how many he saved. No one was interested in numbers, only in seeing him run out over and over into the darkness and then into

Before leading the ill-fated Battle of Ballantyne Pier in Vancouver, Mickey O'Rourke won the Victoria Cross as a stretcher bearer in World War I.
Library and Archives Canada, 3219604

the sunlight defying machine guns and gas and picking up dying men and carrying them back so that they might not die.

After that, after the war, he had trouble working a regular job. The veterans of contemporary wars suffer the same thing. How do you get that out of your mind and sit in an office or work on an assembly line?

Sometimes you don't. Mickey didn't, and he started drinking. That's when I met him. He carried others during the war and afterwards he tried to carry himself and he failed. That was a rescue he could not complete.

And then he led the strikers and was beaten back.

William Foster, the police chief, won what came to be called the Battle of Ballantyne Pier. He never lifted a finger except to point to the strikers and say, "Stop them." Mickey O'Rourke lost the battle. He crawled back to his hotel room and slept.

Mickey died in poverty and obscurity. William died in luxury and fame. He headed several corporations after he retired from the police.

They are both buried in Forest Lawn Cemetery in Burnaby. One difference: Mickey's portrait is hanging in the Canadian War Museum in Ottawa, along with the other Victoria Cross winners.

There is no painting of William Foster there.

In Mickey's portrait he does not have a rifle on his shoulder. He has a stretcher.

RATTENBURY

He was rotten. No two ways about it, he was rotten and nasty and cruel—and you love his work. Strange how life turns out.

I met Francis Rattenbury, who was called Ratz, when he was swimming in praise of his work on the courthouse. You know the place. You now call it the Vancouver Art Gallery, the city's shining temple to creativity and culture, not to mention Hollywood fame.

There is barely a day without cameras and actors milling around the front, with the giant columns and concrete lions. It is the perfect setting for every movie that has a courtroom scene—to get to the scene the pretend lawyers and clients have to go up to the big steps and step inside the room with the judge.

Of course they cannot enter the front because it is sealed off, but going up the stairs is good enough to pretend.

It was a courthouse before it became a home for art. And although Francis Rattenbury designed it he should have been convicted in there for, well, let us see.

Stealing.

Lying.

Being an idiot.

Francis Mawson Rattenbury, architect of the old Vancouver Courthouse, the Empress Hotel and the BC Legislative Buildings, ended his life in a scandalous murder.
Harbour Publishing Archives

Let's start at the beginning. The new, young province of British Columbia wanted a government building in Victoria that would make everyone proud. Something classical. Something like a Roman temple.

Francis Rattenbury, twenty-four years old and studying architecture in England, heard about that. He did not study enough to learn the boring stuff about weights and measures or stress loads or cost ratios, only the fine art of impressing a client.

He was very good at drawing, just not so good at figuring how much his drawings would cost or how they would stand up when they were turned into stone and steel. He drew some beautiful examples of a Romanesque structure, some of which he stole from classmates, and sent them to Victoria.

He did not use his name. He rightly guessed that the judges would not want an English architect. So he signed the presentations as "A BC Architect." That was all. That was humble. That was a lie.

He won the contract. What could be better than a mysterious local man not flaunting his name or hungry for fame?

In the end the parliament building was $400,000 over budget. He stole $50,000 in materials to build his own home. But the building was beautiful.

From that he was given the contract to design the Empress Hotel. Again, beautiful. But while making the Crystal Garden, which is a part of the hotel people remember the most, he was helped by a friend, Percy James. Later Rattenbury refused to give him credit or pay for his work.

Over the years he designed many notable buildings. And then he designed the courthouse on Georgia Street. At the same time he met a pretty young lady named Alma Pakenham. She was beautiful and she was twenty-seven. She had been married twice and found each of those unions not to her liking. He was famous. He was fifty-six and had a wife and two kids.

You can almost predict what happened.

His heart pretended it was young, but it did not have to pretend it was unkind. He left his wife and children and told them to get themselves out of his house. To encourage them to go he turned off the lights and heat. Not nice.

Then he married Alma, who was two years old the first time he promised to love and honour someone else.

There were many who did not like what he did and to escape their criticism the newlyweds sailed to England. They lived in a lovely, fancy house he called Villa Madeira to give it a romantic Italian aura.

But you know what was going to happen. And you are right. Soon Alma

tired of her ancient husband and started an affair with their chauffeur, George Percy Stoner, who was eighteen.

And soon after that Alma and George tiptoed up behind the old fellow while he was reading in a large easy chair and applied a carpenter's hammer to the back of the old head. They did it forcefully.

Alma pleaded guilty to murder. She did it, along with George, she said. But then George pleaded guilty also so Alma said, "Whoops." She didn't really mean to say she did it. It was all George's idea.

The two of them were tried, but Alma was so pretty and apparently appeared so innocent that she was found not guilty. George, on the other hand, was not. He was sentenced to hang until he was dead.

The news in the British tabloids was front page, big headlines, every day. It was reality TV before TV. And then the story got bigger.

Three days after George was found guilty Alma got a dagger and stabbed herself, at least six times, in the chest. The supposition was that there was some remorse.

The wounds were not deep enough to cause permanent damage, so she jumped into a river. It was dramatic enough to be turned into a book and several movies.

And the story continued. The tabloids said the death sentence was unfair to George. They said he was a young man manipulated by an older woman. Alma would have hated that.

More than 300,000 good, upright English people signed a petition to spare his life. And the court did. His sentence was commuted to life in prison.

And the story continues. He was in prison only seven years when there was a need for soldiers to fight in World War II.

"Sign up and go or stay safe in here," George was told.

He signed up and survived and even before the war ended he was married. They later had a daughter and according to those who knew the couple they lived a quiet life.

That would be a nice ending to the story, the kind most of us like.

But no. When George was eighty-four he was accused of indecently assaulting a twelve-year-old boy in a washroom. There goes the nice ending. However, he may have been suffering from Alzheimer's disease and was given a two-year suspended sentence.

As for Ratz, he was put into an unmarked grave. Sixty-five years later a family friend felt sorry for either him or the descendants and put a small headstone on it.

The next time you see someone taking a photo of the parliament building in Victoria, or the Empress Hotel or the Vancouver Art Gallery, go ahead, be tempted to tell them the story. Then think, no they won't believe it.

NELLIE

All the good philosophers and all the good religions and teachers say the same thing: it is not what you say but what you do that counts. Nothing else. (Unless you are talking about Robert Burnaby, who we will talk about later. He proves that even eternally iron-strong laws have loopholes. Sorry.)

But the truth about what you do is what I loved about Nellie Towers. What she did, despite what was done to her, made her a shining star in the dark world of bigotry.

Now let us get to where all the bigotry began in Nellie's life. Unless you have been there it is hard to imagine what it is like hearing a relative screaming at you that "You can't do this to the family!"

And, "What are your children going to look like?"

And, "Don't you care about us? About what we think? I never would have thought YOU would do this to us."

From there it got worse.

There was a time when talking to someone of a different race was frowned on. Having coffee with them resulted in gossip. Going out with them was impossible, unheard of, and don't be stupid.

Marrying one of those people was, "No! Never! You have no right to do this to us, and how could you, and I hate you."

Nellie was born in Saint John, New Brunswick, in 1882. She went to New York for schooling and ended up as a teacher. So far normal and acceptable.

Then one day she was in a jewelry store and behind the counter was Charlie. Let me give it to you quickly. Their eyes met. That has happened to you, right? You know the moment. You feel it right to your feet. There is something unearthly and heavenly when you look at someone's eyes and they look at yours.

Sometimes you just look away and that is the end of it, except you remember those eyes for a while. But then comes the time when, when, you keep looking. And the other person keeps looking. Then one of you looks down in embarrassment and smiles and you both laugh awkwardly.

"Hello, I just came in to have my watch fixed," said Nellie.

"Can I have a look at it?" asked Charlie.

We can skip then next few minutes, which became an hour and a second trip back to the store to pick up the watch and then trying to walk out the door but turning around and going back and asking little questions.

"Have you been here long?"

"Where are you from?"

"Family?"

You know, the usual stuff. And that led to lunch and that led to dinner. And although they were the only mixed couple in the restaurant they did not notice everyone staring at them.

Then the marriage. I knew a mixed couple whose best man did not show up because his family told him not to. Nellie and Charlie got married in 1900. And Nellie's family never spoke to her again and the Catholic Church, in which she had been raised and which was a major part of her life, disavowed her.

Jump ahead and Nellie and Charlie left New York for his home in Vancouver in 1904. They did not notice the stares on the train across the county. They had eyes only for each other—and maybe they peeked at the scenery.

In Vancouver they were the first and only mixed Chinese and white couple in the city. And blessedly they lived in Chinatown, which was much larger than it is now and their neighbours did not seem to care.

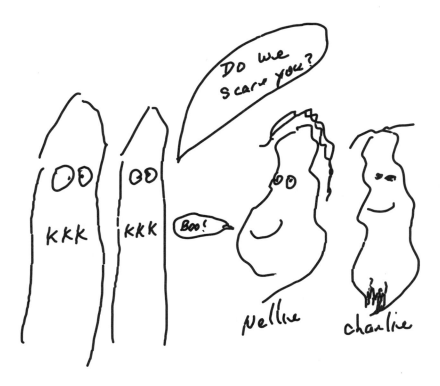

But outside Chinatown the Ku Klux Klan paraded in their white robes through the streets beating up lone Chinese men going to work.

And in 1907, not long after they arrived here, there was the giant anti-Asian riot where hundreds of violent, ugly whites smashed every window of every store in the heart of Chinatown. Thankfully Nellie and Charlie's home was on a side street away from the shops.

I met Nellie when she was older. She was standing in front of her home at 783 East Pender. She was talking with her neighbour in Chinese.

It still is unusual to hear that. It was highly unusual then.

She spoke five dialects. And read Chinese.

But that was just the beginning. It is what you do with things you have that counts and Nellie fought for Chinese residents who were ignored by authorities in every aspect. Shops, government offices, police, she spoke up for them.

And that was only the beginning. She was a midwife and helped give birth to more than five hundred babies in a bedroom of that same house. Those were mothers who could get no care from a hospital.

There was more. Through sheer force of personality and persistence she got Vancouver General Hospital to move its non-white patients out of the basement and onto floors that had windows.

And more. She helped find adoptive families for the babies of single, poverty-stricken women. She was also asked by the Chinese Benevolent Society to be the public nurse for Chinatown.

And one final thing. When the White Lunch restaurant opened it put a sign out front: *No Indians, No Chinese, No dogs*. After Nellie went in the sign came down. Don't mess with Nellie.

During her life she never asked for anything, no pay, not even recognition. She did not have to say a word. She did it all.

She passed away in 1949 at age sixty-seven. Sixty years later city hall put a sign in front of her home as one of the official places that matter in the city.

That is nice.

The plaque says this is an historic place. It is called the Nellie Yip Quong House. It tells about what she did. It is written in both English and Chinese. She would have understood both, but she would have added, "Oh, that's too much fuss to make over me."

AMELIA DOUGLAS

There is nothing too good you can say about James Douglas. He saved this land from being taken over by America. On the other hand, as we have said, he stole the capital from New Westminster. There are some bad words that go with that, if you are living in New West.

But put James aside and let me tell you about Amelia, his wife. There is nothing *but* good about her. No bad at all.

I was surprised when I met her. She was so tiny. Five foot two and eyes of blue, or green, but beautiful. James said he loved them. He was six foot five and 240 pounds. He promised to care for her and protect her, and he did.

They were a mixed couple, and Amelia was already mixed. Her mother was Cree and her father half French Canadian, half Irish. It is crazy now and was crazy then how one little deviation from white can cause so much darkness of thought.

At both Fort Vancouver, in what is now Washington, where she lived with James for ten years, and Fort Victoria on Vancouver Island, where she lived for more than thirty years, she was shunned by the white women.

It is a terrible thing to be isolated. She had her children and her husband, but outside of a few Native women no one would talk to her.

They knew her reputation: kind, loving, a good mother and totally fearless. When she and James were first married James made a big error. He beat to death a Native man who had already murdered someone else, up near Fort St. James.

The dead man's people took offence. The grabbed James in front of his cabin and were about to plunge a knife into his heart when Amelia charged out the front door. She too had a dagger.

The men surrounding her husband laughed at her. They pulled away her weapon.

She ran inside and grabbed every blanket and fur and rug she could find, brought them outside and threw them at the feet of the men. Then she said in her language, "He is just a stupid white man. These are worth more than his life. You can be proud of going home with these treasures. What pride is there in killing one like him?"

There are various reports on what she said exactly, but this is the true one. She told me.

They let her husband go free.

But she could not sway the white women at the trading posts from their bigotry. Not only was Amelia Native, but she was married to a white man, which they said would dilute the entire race. (Actually, James Douglas was mixed but it was hard to tell.)

And they said look at all the children she is having, which they blamed on her. She gave birth to thirteen. Only six survived—which would crush anyone's heart, even in a time when young death was common.

The worst, though, was not from disease but from an accident. Her first son, Alec, was just past the toddler stage when James came back from a long journey. He was so happy to see his son he picked up Alec and threw him into the air, as many fathers do.

There was a scream. Then silence. Alec's neck was broken.

I was there when they buried him. I have never seen, and you would never have seen or felt, such pain and grief. The death of a child is unbearable. The death at your own hands accidentally cannot be imagined, and yet they lived it.

No white women consoled Amelia.

Later, when BC was united as a colony in 1858 and James was promoted to head of the post in Victoria, you'd think that Amelia would be having teas for the ladies whose husbands he was in charge of. That was normal and expected. But of course, no. No teas, no socials, no company other than the women who, like her, no one would talk to. People were nice, but the events were non-events. Amelia devoted herself to helping the poor and sick of Victoria.

And then something happened. James had done such good work saving BC from foreign invaders and Queen Victoria understood the value of that, so in 1863 she knighted him. That gave him the title of Sir James, and Amelia became Lady Amelia.

Suddenly her teas were mandatory. Suddenly those attending had to curtsy to Amelia. Suddenly the tables turned.

And what did Lady Amelia do? She treated all of them with the greatest respect and dignity.

She was the first First Lady of BC and she was the best.

She is buried alongside James in the Ross Bay Cemetery in Victoria.

Opposite:
Amelia Douglas, the first First Lady of BC, never shied away from her Métis heritage and would share ancient Cree legends with all who wanted to hear.
Harbour Publishing Archives

AMOR DE COSMOS

He was crying. That was so sad, and weird, and I did not know what to do to help.

The problem was he was a full grown man with a bushy beard, probably about forty years old, and he was standing on a sidewalk crying.

"Problems?" I asked.

He looked up at me and I knew who and why. He was Amor and he was known for crying—and laughing and fighting and losing his temper and trying to save the world, or at least British Columbia.

That is a lot of tears and angst for one person.

I was in Victoria to cover the swarms of men who were still coming from California to search for gold. While they were here they camped in the parks and generally made a mess of things.

But now there was Amor to talk with, and once he got talking he would not stop.

"I just want people to love each other. Is that too much?" Amor could talk about politics and trade and finances, but his favourite subject was love.

"And I want everyone to get an education, a free education, and I want the loggers and fishermen to get fair pay. And I want men to be able to vote for those in charge."

OK, Amor wanted many things. He was an idealist, which is good. Except don't get him started talking.

He was born Bill Smith in Nova Scotia, but by the time he was in his mid-twenties he was travelling to California looking for gold. But what he was seeing were things others did not see. He saw equality where there was none. And he saw freedoms where there were none. And he saw a change in the direction of his life. The goldfields and streams cared only about one colour, and it was not a skin tone.

In 1854, he legally changed his name to Amor de Cosmos, which he said meant Lover of the Universe. It didn't really, but that's what he said.

He based it on both Latin and Greek, although in Portuguese and Spanish it means "Love of Universe."

Cosmos said, "So what's in a translation? I love order, beauty, the world and the universe."

Period. That was a big period.

He was a little ahead of his time. In the 1970s people I knew changed their names: Judy O'Hagen became Sunshine Moonbeam, and David Brown became Soulfood Basketful, and Maureen Dickson became Maria Sundin, adding to a phonebook full of creativity.

Why not? You can't choose what you look like but you can choose what others call the person who looks like you. You can put your own label on your own brand and be responsible for it yourself.

That was how Amor saw himself. He loved you and he wanted you to know it when you heard his name.

Okay, you think he was a little crazy. But back to his story. He did not find gold in California so he worked his way north to Victoria where he found everything he wanted. He opened a newspaper—the *British Colonist*,

111

in 1858—to fight for the rights of people. He got into politics for the same reason. And he succeeded in many ways.

But what he is mostly remembered for was his name, and his strangeness, and his crying.

"I can't help it," he told me. "Sometimes I see bad things and it makes me cry. Sometimes I see people doing bad things and I have to stop them."

And stopping them often resulted in fist fights, which is not good when you have won an election to represent your people, which he did a number of times, serving in local, provincial and federal roles, or when you become the second premier of BC, which he did in 1872.

Amor de Cosmos made me question things. When we don't understand someone we usually push them away. If you are not like me, if you rub against what I like, then I am not going to pretend I like you. And that just leads to a bad day and a narrow life.

Amor de Cosmos had a profound impact on BC as journalist, premier, Member of Parliament and father of confederation before ending his life in a mental hospital.
Harbour Publishing Archives

Some people don't fit into comfortable moulds, like Smokey Smith, who would not take orders but won the Victoria Cross, and Nellie Towers, who was disowned by her family for marrying someone different but then single-handedly helped several generations of Chinese people in Vancouver.

Don't count people short just because they act differently.

If he was alive today Amor de Cosmos possibly might be diagnosed as manic-depressive. Or he might get some other label.

But he certainly would get help. That was not the case a century ago. He had no friends. He had no family. He had only his dreams of good lives for others and his depression when he did not get them satisfied and his outbursts when he could not control his demons.

At seventy he was declared as being of unsound mind and locked in a mental institution. He died two years later.

He taught me something. The person shouting at you might be saying the right things. Of course it is impossible to care for someone shouting at you, but many of the people who have changed the world have been shouting. And crying.

ROBERT SERVICE

The first time I heard his name I said, "Who?"

That was like being in Rome and saying "Who" when you heard the Pope was coming. But what did I know of a man who wore a suit to work and seldom got rain on his head?

A short time later Robert Service was my number one hero, at least in writing. Terry Fox is my number one hero in life, which beats writing all to heck. More on Terry later.

But now, Robert. He was a bank clerk, not a writer. He spent his days inside a warm, strong building, not in the cold air above icy streams looking for gold.

He counted out money, not scratching through gravel to get it. But without him we would not know the pain, the fear, the joy and the strangeness of the lives of prospectors.

Robert wrote poetry all his life. It was simple poetry, the kind anyone would understand. But there was no money in that. His salary came from a bank.

He came from England in 1896 when he was twenty-one and although he wanted to find gold, as basically everyone in the late 1800s wanted, he got there too late, as basically everyone did.

Without two coins to rub together he arrived in Victoria and got a job in a bank, which within about a year sent him to their outpost in Whitehorse.

Robert Service was a bank teller in Victoria before being transferred to Dawson City, where he gained lasting fame as "the Bard of the Yukon."

John S. Campbell photo, City of Vancouver Archives, AM54-S4-: Port P983

As someone I met along the way said, "There are no wrong turns in life." Robert was alone in a wild town filled with the kind of men he wanted to be but was not. But through the bars of his teller's cage he heard stories that would make his skin tighten and his back stiffen. Unbelievable things happened in the darkness and the cold, all while looking for that stuff called gold.

One night while passing a crowded, noisy saloon, a line, a thought came to him: "A bunch of the boys were whooping it up."

That was all, but it felt good, and it felt like it captured what was happening truthfully and simply, without trying to be literary.

He thought this might become a poem, but the only place he had paper and a pen and a bottle of ink was in the bank. He ran there and just outside it someone fired a shot—probably at him, thinking he was going to rob it.

Maybe it was not that. There were no more shots. But this was a wild town and guns and whiskey and gold made a head-spinning drink.

By morning he had written "The Shooting Of Dan McGrew."

A bunch of the boys were whooping it up in the Malamute saloon;
The kid that handles the music-box was hitting a jag-time tune;
Back of the bar, in a solo game, sat Dangerous Dan McGrew,
And watching his luck was his light-o'-love, the lady that's known as Lou...

It was a love story with two men and one woman and you knew things would not turn out well. But in the story he had the hearts and minds and frozen fingers of those who toiled and moiled for gold. Plus he had the attention of those who wished they were there but could not be there but could read about it.

We are talking so famous that when President Ronald Reagan met Prime Minister Brian Mulroney they recited it, taking alternate verses from memory. Men talking men talk.

However, the woman in the story, Lou, was the winner. When the two men killed each other over her it was Lou who took the poke of gold for herself.

There was also one sidebar to the story that Robert told me about. There was a real Dan McGrew in Whitehorse whose nickname was Dangerous Dan. He and Dan did not get along. Once Robert said one day he would kill Dan.

He did it with his pen.

Later Robert heard another story through the bank teller's bars that made him feel like he was in prison. It came from a miner down from Dawson City, the furthest of all the golden outposts.

(I met a fellow there once when I was doing some reporting about life in the north. He had a nugget the size of a Zippo cigarette lighter. This was in the days when there were cigarettes and lighters, but believe me, the lighter was large. He took the nugget out of his pants pocket. It filled the palm of his hand. I said, "Aren't you afraid someone might steal it?"

He looked at me, then cast his eyes around the vastness of everything around us and said, "And where would he go?")

Through the bars of his teller's cage Robert heard the story of a miner whose partner died. The miner could not dig a grave in the frozen earth so he cremated him.

Robert spent the night walking in the cold and telling the story over and over in his mind.

In the morning he wrote "The Cremation of Sam McGee."

What I learned from Robert is that when know your story back to front and inside and out, as some say, it writes itself. There is no pain with the pen. Or, if you insist, with the keyboard, but I still prefer dipping the end of a pen in a bottle of ink. That is magic not known with plastic buttons.

Robert sent those and other poems to his father in Toronto to have them turned into a small booklet to give away to friends at Christmas. He sent a cheque to pay for it.

But while they were being set in type the printers started reciting the poems. There was nothing else so down to earth and easy to understand.

Along with Robert's father the printer sold 1,700 copies just of the galley proofs, which means not a book but just the raw pages before they were all bound together.

His father sent back the cheque and Robert's slim and plain booklet was no more. It was a full-sized handsome book that went through seven printings before its official release date.

The reason: the stories, the poems, were real and easy to understand, and easy to read and then memorize and wonderful to tell and tell again.

Robert, who also volunteered as an ambulance driver in World War I, died a happy and wealthy man at eighty-four, in a comfortable and warm home in Lancieux, France.

One of his many obituaries said that he was "the people's poet."

Now it was before he died, obviously, that I confessed to Robert that I did not recognize his name.

"No problem," he said. "I bet many people don't know yours." Then he added, "Do you know my poems?"

"Yes, of course, I've heard them over and over and even know some by heart."

"Did you see that most of the men in my stories died a harsh death?"

"Yes."

"Do you remember their names?"

"Yes."

"Then I'm happy. I will depart in peace while those around me will talk about Sam McGee, who did not. Can't ask for more." Then he gave me a challenge. "You are a reporter, right? Why don't you use some imagination in your stories."

So I tried. There is a story about Kitsilano Beach that you might know. It was once Greer's Beach, and then came the railroad and a battle and a gun shot.

And one thing more, too hard to rhyme: they got his name off the beach, but leading to it is a street with the name Greer.

I, Jock Linn, am not a Robert Service. But here are my notes on Greer, and the beach:

SAM Greer
From Ireland
Nicknamed Gritty —
Because he was

Went to The US
+
Fought in Civil War —

on the side of The North —
survived

came To B.C. —

The Legend of Samuel Greer

The moon was cold upon the beach
When Sam said to the CPR,
This sand is beyond your thieving reach.
Go steal some other dusty land.

Sam bought the land years before
And had a deed that said it was so.
But the CPR wanted every inch
And the railroad said it would not flinch.
On that beach they would build a resort.
But Sam said no. We can go to court.
The city sent a sheriff.
Sam said go lay an egg.

He fired a shotgun through his door
And struck the sheriff in the leg.

He was sent to prison for two years,
And his loving friends were in tears.
They protested and he was soon let free,
But not before his home was a memory.

The railroad renamed it Kits,
But the hotel idea fell to bits.
And on a cold night when the moon is high,
If you look near where the basketballs fly,
You might see an angry son of a gun
In front of a home where he took his stand,
A home paid for and built with his own hand.

118

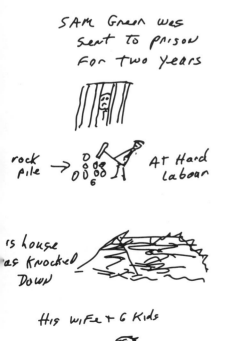

JOHN L. SULLIVAN

"Gawd, that was awful. The worst performance ever."

"Shhhhsh. You're right. His acting stinks, but be quiet."

And then the final curtain.

"Cheers. Bravo. The Best, Ever." The applause went on for minute after minute after minute. It seemed like it would never stop—then it tapered off, but did not stop.

"Isn't he wonderful," said a woman.

"The best!" said a man.

And who? Well, John L. That would be John L. Sullivan to you but we called him John L. along with the rest of the civilized world. And everyone knew who John L. was.

The toughest, meanest, most fearless man alive. The last of the great bare-knuckle boxers. The champion of the world.

There was no dancing around for John L. Sullivan. At the bell he would take four steps to the middle of the ring and face his opponent and start punching. There was no grace about it. No floating like a butterfly. It was just brutal pounding of a fist into the face and body and being pounded upon.

And there was no relief after exhaustion. No ten-round matches. He once took seventy-five rounds to knock out his opponent. And if he didn't do it then, they still had five rounds to go.

120

A fight could last two hours and a few times they did, in the rain.

For a few years John L. toured across the country with a dozen other boxers fighting every night in every town, either with each other or taking on all comers. He drank and he boxed and he drank and boxed. It was a simple regimen. He won the heavyweight boxing title in 1882. He was also the first athlete to earn more than a million dollars.

In his professional career he had fifty-one fights. He lost one, and that was at the end of his career. That was after the rules changed and he fought with gloves.

And now that he was retired he wanted a new career. He would be an actor. And tonight, on January 8, 1892, he was on stage at the Vancouver Opera House on Granville Street.

The newspapers had warned the crowds that he was little better than the trained animals that were big on the vaudeville stage, but they did not care. They went deep in their pockets to get tickets.

He was John L. and that was good enough for them. Just to see him, even forgetting his lines and forgetting to face the actors he was talking to and forgetting to leave the stage after the scene ended did not matter. He was John L. The applause went on and on.

John L. loved Vancouver. He came back numerous times. He coached young boxers at the Vancouver Athletic Club and refereed matches and even umpired a baseball game.

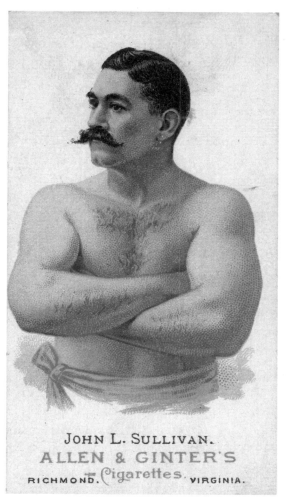

JOHN L. SULLIVAN.
ALLEN & GINTER'S
RICHMOND. Cigarettes. VIRGINIA.

As I said, he drank a lot but on this night when I went to see him we were promised that he would be kept sober before his appearance. There would be no uncalled-for scenes, we were told, which often happened. And at the end there would be no speech.

Once, in San Francisco, he told the audience: "I know I ain't no actor but I gets the money just the same, see!"

It is hard to love someone when they are insulting you. On the other hand, we were all paying to see him be himself and we felt a little cheated that he was respectable.

And he almost became a permanent resident. He spent $10,000 for property in Point Grey, but it just sat there waiting for his return.

There was a group of us reporters hanging around wherever he went. It was one saloon, or another saloon, or let's see, the Hollow Tree in Stanley Park, and then another saloon.

He told us he had been coming to Vancouver for years and he said he could kick himself for not investing in more real estate. Little did he know he was a fortune teller.

"I knew this place when it was little more than a fish camp, and I knew it would grow big."

See, fortune teller.

Seventeen years after his first performance at the Vancouver Opera House John L. was back playing the Pantages Theatre. Hundreds were turned away each night and the police had a hard time keeping control of the crowds.

Do you remember the Pantages Theatre? What?! Peter Pantages was almost as popular as John L. and he never punched anyone in the nose.

PETER PANTAGES

It was so different in those days. Can you imagine East Hastings without the drugs and decay and crime and overwhelming ugliness? I wish you did not have to imagine it, but if you were alive a hundred years ago you would have seen sights that would have made you proud to be alive, especially in this city.

Restaurants squeezed between clothing shops and newsstands. Crowds on the street all dressed for work or dining or shopping and streetcars pushed through the Model T traffic, mostly jitney cabs that would take you home for a nickel.

And there were the theatres, many of them, but especially the Pantages.

There were no bad seats in the house. The sightlines were so good that you could see everything from anywhere and the acoustics, well just imagine in this age of blasting mega speakers that a simple voice talking from the stage could be heard in the back row of the balcony. That is if everyone was quiet, and they usually were—except when John L. was there.

It was next door to the Carnegie Library where half the kids in the city did their homework and waited while their mothers went shopping at Woodward's.

The theatre was built in 1907 by Alexander Pantages, an immigrant from Greece at a time when many Greeks were coming here. The stage held song and dance routines and some plays. But this is not about the entertainment but about a kid who worked there.

He was Peter Pantages, nephew of Alexander, newly arrived from Greece with instructions to go directly to the theatre: "Tell your uncle you are there and go to work."

On the way to work one day the teenager made a wrong turn. He wound up at English Bay. He grew up near water in Greece and here was water in this new home. "I think I'm going to like it," he said to himself, or at least that's what he told me he said.

He stripped off his pants and shirt and in his underwear ran straight in.

The he said something else. "Owww," Rather: "OWWW!! THIS IS COLD!" I know he said that because he laughed when he told me. He said it in Greek and English and several other unknown languages.

Water in Greece was warm.

"But it was still water," he said, "and I loved it. It will just take a little getting use to."

From that day on he was at the beach every day. When it was sunny and hot, when it was raining and cold. When it was snowing. When he felt happy, he was there. When he felt sad, something I never saw him being, but he said when he was sad he was in the water.

And when someone finds something they love, whether it is religion or swimming or yogurt, they want to do more of it. So Peter started swimming three times a day. Every day. Year-round.

No, honestly, I never figured out how he managed, but when you really want to do something, no matter what, you do it. There is a great philosophy of life in that.

And then came the New Year's Eve party at his home, about a decade later. That was the dawn of 1920. Everyone wore their finest. There were tuxedos and high hats and slinky dresses on beautiful women.

I know you might find this hard to believe but I took off my cap and rented a top hat for the occasion. And a tux. It felt so stiff. And yes, of course I was there. If I wasn't how would I be able to tell you this?

About three in the morning, when the alcohol and excitement had slowed down, Peter made an announcement: "I would like everyone to join me in the morning for a dip in the bay."

"Whaatttt??" Everyone looked at everyone and everyone had an open mouth and wide open eyes and suddenly sober heads.

"Noooo!" said everyone, and that was everyone, at least everyone who had not sneaked upstairs to sleep in any bed they could find.

"Seriously, it will be good for you," said Peter.

"No, it won't," said everyone.

But the idea was secretly exciting. It would be a New Year's not to forget.

The rest of the night was spent thinking about the morning and shortly after the sun was up Peter gathered everyone who was awake and woke everyone who had passed out and said off to the beach we go.

There are pictures of this. Top hats, dresses, pants that are not rolled up in the water. There were screams. There was laughter. There were giggles. There were no towels. Who in our condition would have thought of doing something sensible when what we were doing was crazy?

We shivered, we laughed and in dribs and drabs we went home, mostly to hot baths.

The next year we were back, along with a small crowd that heard about the insane Polar Bear Swim.

Except for the year of the pandemic, it has been held every New Year's morning since then. And even in the pandemic there were those who broke the rules.

Peter was a cool guy.

Opposite: Restaurateur Peter Pantages, a scion of the famous movie theatre family, created the annual Polar Bear Swim and was the president of the club for fifty-one years.
Stuart Thomson photo, City of Vancouver Archives, AM1535-: CVA 99-1503

FONCIE PULICE

All we have now are selfies. Here I am in front of whatever this is. And here I am here and here and here. And here I am over there, by myself.

Foncie would say you are so indulgent it's embarrassing. A photo of you should be special, should be rare, and if you had only one or two they would have meaning.

"Here I was in my army uniform. Here, my son, my daughter, here I was on my first date with your mother. That was so long ago."

"Did you really look like that?" says the son/daughter. Then they think: "I hope I don't look like you when I'm old."

That is the value of a photo. Just one moment you remember, not hundreds you forgot.

Foncie took my picture during the Depression when no one could afford a camera. And certainly no one could afford going to a studio for a professional photo.

Foncie's studio was on the street. He would see you coming, smile at you and click. And there you were forever. I still have that picture and, well of course I haven't changed, but of the millions of other pictures he took every later one was different.

That was history you and your family could understand. Things change. People change. The clothes we wore changed. Yes, especially the clothes.

In every Foncie picture the people walking on Granville or Hastings

Street were well dressed. Most were going shopping or meeting someone for tea or coming from work. No torn jeans to be seen.

Even the loggers were dressed as best they could be, even while working. That sounds strange, but it was true. They would put on a jacket before going into the woods. It was tough material. They would take it off before climbing onto the spring boards, but there was no other way of looking except good.

Things change. Time changes. And you learn it from the photos, mostly Foncie's Fotos.

It might have been his name that helped him. Alfonse Pulice, shortened to Foncie, which fits nicely with Fotos. But really it was just that he was a good person. That counts by any name. And he smiled. And he worked hard.

Twenty-year-old Foncie was painting houses in 1934 when he saw others taking pictures on the street. That looked a lot more fun than climbing a ladder with a brush and pail.

He went to work for an old time photographer, and he did well. His first assignment was at Main and Hastings, which was the Times Square of Vancouver. Everyone passed by here on their way to shopping at Woodward's or learn-

ing things at the Carnegie Library. Foncie's job was just stand on the corner and for each person he could take a full-sized picture, shoes to hat, and give them a ticket and say they could get a print the next day for twenty-five cents.

Not a bad deal. No one had a camera of their own. He took thousands of pictures and life was good. Then came the war and Foncie went off to fight.

When he came back he married his teenage sweetheart, Anne. They put all their money together and bought a camera, and Foncie went to work. He was out all day and into the night. When it was dark he moved under the lights of the theatres of Granville Street and kept taking pictures.

Anne was in their tiny studio a few blocks away. The studio changed locations many times but the process was always the same. She would process the film at night and print the pictures.

The next day customers would come with their slips of paper and pick up a picture. She was sweet and thanked everyone and they were happy.

This went on as the people in the pictures had children and the children had children and every time they would go out for dinner at the Peter Pan Café (run by Peter Pantages, you just read about him) or to the PNE or to Stanley Park they would look for Foncie to get a photo.

He worked from 1935 to 1979. The only real time off was when he was in the army. He worked six days a week and seldom took a vacation. And he loved it. He laughed. He greeted every potential customer with a happy face. Who would not like that?

And again, when they picked up their pictures, Anne smiled and thanked them. That is the entire Harvard Business School in two smiles.

But everything ends. By the late 1970s everyone had a camera. Anne and Foncie retired to Kelowna and lived happily with their children and grandchildren and took pictures of them.

You want to see Vancouver as it really was in the 1930s and '40s and '50s and '60s and '70s, see how it changed, see how people were before some streets became war zones and sidewalks became slums where photographers have bottles thrown at them, look up Foncie's Fotos. You will feel good. And it will be more than just a holy cow experience. It will be a time warp.

IVY
GRANSTROM

The strange thing about Ivy was not that she was running so fast, it's that she was pulling an anchor.

She was at the track across the street from VanDusen Gardens on Oak Street and I was doing a television story about her. I had gone from a quill pen to 16-mm film.

Moving pictures did one thing that the pen could not. When I wrote that Ivy ran fast you had no idea how fast. When you saw her running, when the other reporters and editors saw how fast she was running, they said: "I can't believe how fast she is running." But there she was, running that fast, right in front of their eyes.

And right in front of her eyes was something that Ivy could not say. She was blind. She only knew she was running faster than the fellow she was tied to with a rope. He was not pulling her. She was pulling him.

The rule for a blind runner in official competition was that the blind person had to be ahead of the person who was making sure they would stay on the track.

Now think about that. How can someone guide you when they are behind you? Okay, shouting. But try that when in full-bore running and breathing is being done in industrial-sized ins and outs—talking is not part of either of those.

And so Ivy was pulling her partner, and she could have gone faster. That's what she said.

Ivy was simply your typical outstanding, incredibly unbelievable and lovable and wonderful and sweet blind woman. She was born with poor sight that continued to get worse.

Still, during World War II she trained as a nurse with the Red Cross. She hid her bad sight. Again, how do you do that? You have endless reading to do, which she did with her face just above the books, and hiding because she did not want anyone to know.

And there were the bandages and the measuring of everything and the charts that needed filling out. Somehow she did it.

And then someone noticed what she was doing and she was no longer a nurse. So she got a job as a waitress. How do you do that with bad eyes? But she did. Up until she was sixty Ivy did just amazing.

Then her world ended. She was a passenger in a car when suddenly

there was a terrible crash. Her back was injured so badly doctors told her she would spend her life in a wheelchair.

She blurted out a bad word. A really bad word, something she did not do.

Over the next few years she took up walking. Every step was painful. Then jogging. The same with every step. Then running. By now forget the pain, she was either overcoming it or wearing it away.

Eight years later she joined a masters competition and won medal after medal at the Masters Athletics World Championships and Masters Games.

It was in this period that I saw her training, pulling that weight behind her. "I could go faster, you know," she said to me.

131

"I know."

She ran off and I added, "If only we could all follow you."

Let us hang a few more decorations around her neck:

She was named the Sports BC Athlete of the Year in 1982, appointed to the Order of Canada in 1988, and is a member of the BC Sports Hall of Fame and the Canadian Disability Hall of Fame. All of this while totally blind.

And let us not forget the Polar Bear Swim. For seventy-six consecutive years she was in the cold water, and stayed in longer than most others.

The last time I saw her there I could not see her. She was surrounded by hundreds of people who loved her. She was famous, at least for a while. She could not see them, but she heard them, calling her the "Queen of the Polar Bears."

I saw her shortly after she got dried off and was walking up to Davie Street where she would get a ride home.

"I am so happy," she said.

One last honour: in 2001 she was inducted into the Terry Fox Hall of Fame.

Up in heaven it is hard to know which one of them is more thrilled to meet the other.

As if being blind wasn't hard enough, ex-nurse Ivy Granstrom lost the use of her legs in a car crash. But she rehabbed until she could run, and ran her way into the BC Sports Hall of Fame.

City of Vancouver Archives, AM1533-S2-4-: 2009-005.574

TERRY FOX

Yes, he is my hero. There is no one else I have ever met who made me know how far a human being can go without complaining, despite having everything to complain about.

I was lucky—no, I was honoured—to interview Terry shortly before he died.

Now, please accept the fact that after a century of extended existence my appearance has changed. I lost hair and gained weight. I was hardly recognizable, even to myself. Every day I look in a mirror and say, "Who's that?" But it's me.

But looks were not important that day in the hospital. The camera was on Terry the entire time. He was propped up on a pillow and he talked of how he wished he was still on the road and how bad he felt that he had quit.

I asked about the pain. He had it on every step. It was on his face with every step.

The grimace and then the twitch that came when his stump hit the mechanical leg. Every step up to ten times a minute, thirty minutes at a time before he would take a break and walk for a few steps. Then he would jerk his body back up to the running stride and use the strength to make the step and hop and run and step and hop and run and step and hop. It is hard to write, hard to read, and always with the pain.

"That's not important," he said.

Terry Fox's goal was to get at least one dollar from every Canadian for cancer research. To date the Terry Fox Foundation has raised over $800 million.

Harbour Publishing Archives

We talked about the courage he gave to others with cancer.

"That makes me feel good. But I wish I could have gone on."

It was his only wish, that after he had given everything that he could have given more.

We talked about death.

"There's nothing to be afraid of and whatever happens will be on God's hands."

That was peace without concern. That was fulfillment without expectation.

His wish was to help. His actions accomplished what he wanted even though he did not believe he accomplished it.

There was no self pity, no complaint, no self praise, no wish to be remembered.

As we talked his neck and then his cheeks turned slowly red. After running halfway across the country with an artificial leg he was exhausted by lying in bed talking.

He closed his eyes to sleep, just sleep.

We stopped the camera and took down the light and silently left the room.

There should be a statue of Terry in front of the Parliament Buildings in Ottawa and everyone going in should look at it, every day. They might consider running with him.

HARRY AOKI

How do you study music through correspondence? Honestly, the notes are written and the notes are corrected. But what about the tone—the vibes, as they say—the soul of the sound?

You can't do that on a handwritten note sent in the mail to a school in another country.

Or, of course you can. Because you can do anything, under any conditions, at any time, with basically nothing.

Harry Aoki was born in Canada and so he was a citizen of Canada. When World War II came around, as wars seem to have a way of coming, the Japanese were the enemy, along with the Germans.

You notice that the Japanese and the Germans are Canada's close allies today. Politics, war and hate are insane, but we humans keep thinking wars will save us. Be careful of who you hate, your children will probably marry them.

And in that war, as you know, suddenly all people who were Japanese, or looked Japanese, or had some Japanese ancestry, were enemies. That included people who were Canadian, who looked Japanese.

It should have been illegal, and was immoral, but what the heck, we did it anyway.

This fear did not include people who were German or who were German descendants living here, even though we were dropping bombs on them in

Germany. The difference was Germans were white. The Japanese were not. That is an extremely simple answer to an extremely complex question.

The RCMP came for Harry and everyone else who looked like Harry. There were posters everywhere: NOTICE TO ALL JAPANESE PERSONS AND PERSONS OF JAPANESE RACIAL ORIGIN.

Can you imagine being Japanese—no, being Canadian with Japanese parents—and seeing this? Fear, and worse, terror, confusion, pain. More words, but they all meant "Why? I did nothing wrong."

We see the pictures of Jews in Germany wearing the Star of David badges. The same in Canada, without the badges but add a racist twist. The Germans here were free, the Japanese were not. Not hard to understand that.

The RCMP came and knocked on doors in Steveston and Ladner and in Japantown in Vancouver. They knocked hard. This was not a polite "Are you home?" knock. It was a pounding of a fist with a leather glove. Hard. It scares you.

You opened the door and there was no greeting. There was a frightening police officer and his first words were "You have to leave. Now."

Then: "You have five minutes to gather your belongings and you can take only one small bag."

Panic. For everyone, what to take, where are you going, and why?

For the heads of the houses, where are the marriage certificate, the mortgage, the family pictures, the cash we saved? Hurry.

For the mothers, where are the baby clothes, the linens, the wedding dress, tomorrow's clothes for everyone else?

For Harry, where is my violin? Harry was a musician. He also played the piano, but that would be out of the question, obviously. Forget it. Just grab the violin, which he loved more than anything.

"Too big," said the RCMP.

I was there on the street when Harry's hands went cold. "I need my violin." That is all he said, but what he thought, what was in his mind, in his heart, was that life without his violin was life without air and water. There was nothing I could do. The insane government was slamming down its mindless hand.

His violin was too big. What an absurdity. How can a violin be too big?

He ran back into his home, after the cruel, merciless time was up, and grabbed a harmonica. Not too big.

I cried. I hate to say that, but I cried. Harry was so good and was treated so badly. Like so many others.

For almost five years he lived in internment camps, first in Blind Bay in the Shuswap at a logging camp and then with his family at a sugar beet camp in Alberta—all far enough from the coast so this former violin player would not be a threat to Canada. Camps with rows of stark wooden hollow shacks that housed despair and confusion, heartbreak.

Heartbreak is such an overused word. Just say cold tears. Why am I here?

Following the attack on Pearl Harbor all 21,000 BC coast residents of Japanese descent were detained and relocated inland. Families were split up and men billeted in the PNE Forum.

Harbour Publishing Archives

Harry played his harmonica. He did the work at camp that he was ordered to do and he grew the food that he and others would eat and he played. He played to make others happy. He played to encourage others. He played to make them forget.

And he took a correspondence course at the University of Chicago in music theory. Can you give Canada credit for allowing this? Well, yes, of course. It was not so in Germany. Can you condemn Canada for allowing this? Yes, when you consider it should not have been a question to allow him to write letters.

Back to the original question: how do you study music by letter? I don't know. But Harry did.

And after the war Harry Aoki played Mozart on his harmonica with the Calgary Philharmonic Orchestra. Can't beat that. And he spent the rest of his life working to use music to overcome everything.

Harry was a Canadian. But maybe more than that he was a soul who would not be conquered.

"$1.49 DAY, WOODWARD'S"

Y ou have your favourite song. Everyone does. You know the words. You sing along.

And of course, you saw by the title, that THE most favourite song in Vancouver and New West and Burnaby and well, everywhere, up until near the end of the 1900s was "$1.49 Day, Woodward's."

You just sang it. I know. So did I.

Or if you are a latecomer to the planet and BC, you've never heard of it. Pity, you missed one of the great cultural events of the century.

Let's go right to it. A whistled tune, then *dollar forty-nine day, Woodward's*. Then another whistle.

That is great writing. No kidding. Great writing is what people remember and repeat. *Somewhere over the rainbow... I left my heart, in San Francisco... Dollar forty-nine day...*

Please, if you don't know about it ask your mother. If she is young, ask your grandmother. Ask your neighbour. Ask anyone who went shopping in the 1950s, or '60s, or '70s, or '80s, or the very early '90s.

But not after that. It does not seem that long ago to me, but that is because ships with sails and taking a bath once a week were not that long ago either.

When you get older you will understand.

Charles Woodward established the first Woodward's store at the corner of Main and Georgia Streets in Vancouver in 1892. In time the business expanded to eighteen stores and became the largest retailer in western Canada before winding down in 1993.

City of Vancouver Archives, AM54-S4-: Bu P704

Tony Antonias worked in radio when radio was king, and all the princes served inside its realm.

There was no television, thank goodness. Stories came from voices out of the box and you could understand them. They were not so fast and with so many edits you could not blink between sentences. In fact, they *used* sentences. They don't now.

Watch one of those idiotic TV commercials about anything and there are ten edits in three seconds and four words, none saying anything but buy and buy. In high speed.

But back then there was music and the DJs, the disc jockies, were the most famous people in the province.

Advertising was done by word, not an actor with a white coat standing in front of a model of a tooth saying, "If it's not white enough buy our whitening paste and in a week you will be the happiest person on earth." And when it doesn't work you watch the next person with a tooth saying, "Our paste is not like those other pastes, this will make you happy."

No, sir. In radio, they had to sing, "You'll wonder where the yellow went, when you brush your teeth with Pepsodent."

You can see the difference.

Okay, I can't either. But the radio had to hold you without a picture. And jingle writers got paid more than news writers, so therefore they must have been smarter.

I met Tony in 1958. He worked for CKNW, which was then, still is, the big station. They called themselves the Top Dog, which in the '50s and '60s were understandable words to those who listened to Hound Dog on the radio.

If you have to ask, please look it up. It was the rap of your ancestors.

Tony Antonias wrote jingles for the station's advertisers. There were no pictures, as we said, so Tony would come up with a cute little line about the product. He did hundreds, maybe thousands.

He got to be the chief of the creative department—pretty nifty, as they said then.

And he wanted one thing. If he was going to spend his days pounding out silly little words he needed a new typewriter. The one he had was nicotine stained, and he did not smoke. It was ancient. He had to reset the ribbon every time it came to the end.

Your eyes are closing. What is a ribbon?

It was the strip of ink-soaked half-inch (don't ask what is a half-inch) ribbon that went between the metal keys with letters on them and the paper on which an impression of the letter would be left.

You got it. Like typing on your laptop except each letter is individually hammered onto the paper and if you mess up you are in trouble. And when your ribbon runs out of ink you have to change it. And no one on earth was ever able to do that without getting ink all over both hands. And that was ink that did not come off with just one washing.

There was more. When the spool—yes, the ribbon was wound on spools at each side of the typewriter—when the spool came to the end it would automatically switch back and go the other way.

Except Tony's did not. And he wanted a new machine.

He went on vacation and said when he came back that if he did not have new typewriter he would quit.

Management did not want that, so they got him a new typewriter, on which the ribbon automatically changed direction. And Tony was happy.

Then they told him his first job back from a good rest was to do something creative for $1.49 Day.

No!! $1.49 Day had been around for years. It was always the same. Call the store, get a list of things that would be on sale and list them on the radio.

"No!" said Tony. "That's a job for someone down the ladder. Someone who is learning the business. I am the boss."

"Do it, or you can find a typewriter somewhere else," he was told.

He walked back to his desk in the large copy-writing room. He was depressed. Did they not care about him? Was all his work worth nothing?

A group of younger jingle writers were standing around his new machine, admiring it.

"Wish I could have one like this."

Yes. Most of us wish for new things.

"I could write better if I had one like this."

No. You could write better if you learned how to write. It is not the tools, it is the tool handler. But you know this.

Tony looked at the machine, then in anger jabbed the keys.

BING!

What was that? He jabbed again. *Bing.* Jabbed again, and again. *Bing, bing.* Some said it was *ding, ding, ding.* You take your pick. *Ding, bing.* It was something that made a sound.

New technology. The machine had a bell that would ring when you were five strokes away from the end of the line. You could either squeeze in a word or throw the carriage return and go to the next line.

Before electric typewriters you had to push a lever from left to right to advance to the beginning of the next line. Every line, in every story. Most people just threw it across, *zip, bang*. No bell, just the *thud, bang* of a piece of steel thudding and banging.

Every story in every book in every newspaper in every movie script and every jingle was written this way during the early twentieth century. That's a lot of throwing. And no one knew when they were coming to the end of the line, so you would have the beginning of a word that ran out of space before you could finish it.

Now the bell. But Tony was not thinking of that. He was an artist. *Ding, ding, ding. Bing, bing, bing.*

"As God is my witness," he later told me, "I heard a melody. I sat down and wrote: "$1.49 Day, Woodward's. $1.49 Day, Tuesday."

Great writing does not have to be lengthy.

Tony went home happy, but the more he thought about it he knew it was not finished. Back at the radio station the next day he jokingly added a whistle of his own. It was recorded and put at the beginning and end of the words, which were sung, or chanted, by two voiceover men.

That was February 17, 1958. The jingle was on the air at the start of every week until the store closed in 1993. That is thirty-five years of a two-line hit.

A few years after the jingle first aired, the Hollywood Advertising Club gave Tony an award for "World's Best Broadcast Advertising."

And no, Tony did not get paid anything extra for it.

But he told me his big reward was when the station got a call from a health facility in New Westminster. They wanted to let the people at CKNW know about a little boy who had never opened his mouth, never said a word in his life, until he heard the $1.49 Day jingle on the radio and started singing it.

Bing! Ding!

A child speaks. A jingle is sung. A silly little slogan is remembered and a memory is forever.

THE MEDAL

Sometimes people just do good things and you have to say to yourself there is hope. There was no reason for them to do what they did, and yet, they did it.

Start with Brandon Kuczynski, who has a hobby of searching for lost treasures in the ground. He uses a metal detector, which was developed in wartime to detect hidden land mines that would blow off a soldier's legs if he stepped on one.

How utterly, painfully ugly. The enemy did not stay and fight, he hid his evil and fled. There is no battlefield honour in that.

So someone worked on an instrument that could sense metal under the ground and send a signal to a soldier holding it that something was where it should not be.

Then the soldier, and this was one of the worst assignments to have in any army, would kneel where the signalling beep was coming from and carefully poke at it with a long knife until he felt the hardness of it. And then so carefully dig around it until he could lift it out of the ground.

Unless he disturbed it.

And then the next soldier with the next metal detector would replace him and keep looking, below the ground, for things they could not see that they had to find, while wishing they had any other assignment. But if they did not find them they knew someone would be in a wheelchair for the rest of their life.

These godforsaken things are still buried in countries where there are no more wars but where children play. As a species we have not done well.

On the other hand there are good people, like Brandon. He used the very same life-saving tool to find treasures, rings, coins, pull tabs from beer cans—it is a great hobby.

He was with a friend and his fiancée in Chilliwack in a field where once there was a school. His machine went *beep, beep, beep.*

This was good. No explosions under the mud and grass. He dug and shouted, "What is this?"

It was a dirty silver coin, bigger than an old silver dollar. It had a man on horseback on one side and a picture of a king on the other. On the edge was a name: *C. Whittle.* This was a good find.

It turned out to be King George V, and the coin was a medal.

At that moment Brandon knew he had something worth a great deal. How much? Thousands of dollars?

But he never thought of that. He had only one thought. "I wanted to give it back to whoever owned it," he told a much different looking me. Again, you would never recognize me from the old days.

He spent a year trying to trace the medal back to whomever. He learned it was a medal for service and given to a nurse named Carolyn Whittle. He tracked her family all over the country.

But if you ever try to find someone who you don't know by other than just a name, and you have nothing else to go on, you will say, "Can't go on. Stuck. Don't know where to turn."

We put his story on television. It was touching and kind and a mystery.

Watching television that night was Marion Robinson in Mission. Many of us have hobbies. Marion's is digging into records and finding things. It is much harder than digging into the ground.

Within a few days she had found that Carolyn Whittle had not only been a nurse in World War I, but a front line nurse. This was someone extraordinary. Women were not there where men were being blown apart. Nurses, for all their endless endurance of treating and easing the pain of dying men, were in the hospital tents with the blood and the screams, where they were needed.

Somehow Carolyn was in the trenches. We don't know how. We do know that is where she was. And we know the medal was given not just for service, but for valour.

Marion also learned through her amazing research that Carolyn was engaged to a soldier back then. They had their prenuptial bans read in a church. When the fighting was over they would wed.

Then her husband-to-be was hit by a bullet. He died in a trench.

After the war, she was presented with the British War Medal by a truly grateful government. Then she became a nun. There would be no other men for her.

To be a nun she had to give away all her earthly belongings, including the silver medal. She gave it to her sister, who gave it to her son, who took it to school for show and tell. And he lost it. Things happen. You show it to someone else and then someone else wants to see it and it gets jostled and it falls out of your hand into some bushes and no matter how hard you look, you can't find it.

It happens.

And eighty years later after the school is gone Brandon comes along with his treasure-hunting instrument and *beep, beep, beep.*

Marion traced Carolyn Whittle to the Caribbean, where her order sent her to set up an orphanage. And there she treated a disease that later was named polio. There was no vaccine. She rubbed the legs of the children who could not walk with oils and she rubbed and rubbed, and almost like a miracle—no, not almost, it was a miracle—some did walk again.

She worked until her health was gone. She was sent to a convent to rest and regain her strength, and then sent to Colorado, where she was told to set up another hospital and again, treat the untreatable.

She should have been given a duffle bag full of medals.

And Marion traced Carolyn's closest living relation to a retirement home in Chilliwack, where Lois Maurer, age ninety-five, was living. She was the daughter of Carolyn's sister. She was younger than her brother. She did not get to take the medal to school to show and tell. She had never met her aunt Carolyn.

But in a parking lot in front of the Birchwood retirement home in Chilliwack on a chilly Sunday morning Brandon gave the silver medal to Lois. He'd bought a box from a coin shop and placed the medal in it.

Lois donated it to the Chilliwack Museum.

And it was discovered by a machine that was meant to counteract a heartless evil. It is a hard world to understand. Luckily we have Lois, Brandon and Marion on the good side, and especially Carolyn.

CURTIS'S TREE

There are so many simply good people. And there are so many who are not.

That is the yin-yang of everything. One pulling one way, the other the other way. For every bad thing that happens there is something good. Sometimes it is hard to see, like with the tree.

It was dark night in March 1997. Curtis Giesbrecht was driving home when his car suddenly went dead. He pulled over to the side of Highway 1 near 160th Street. He was well off the road.

He put on his blinkers, as he should. He got out to open the hood and see if it was possible to do anything.

And then a driver who was doing everything wrong, not paying attention, not awake, we don't know, just that it was everything wrong, he saw the blinking lights and drove at full speed right into them.

In a blink, in something so quick you can't realize it, in something that ended twenty-two years of growing and loving and wanting and hoping and working and dreaming and wishing and working some more, Curtis was dead.

No sense in describing the accident. Terrible, horrible, unspeakable. It happened.

Go past the shrieks of learning about it, past the initial pain, past the lingering depression, past the dinners and holidays and ordinary days that were empty. So many suffer this way. But we go past that.

And wait a year. And then Curtis's parents, Ethel and Larry, with Curtis's little sister Maria planted a small tree near the spot where Curtis left the earth. It was illegal, of course, so they did it quickly and left.

Let a year go by and two fellows driving home from work near Christmastime saw the tree. They were Dan Erika and Chris Angelia. They worked together in a heavy-lifting job.

"That tree looks so lonely," said Dan.

"We should do something about it," said Chris.

The next day they brought some decorations and on their way home pulled over to the side of the highway and put balls and plastic ribbons on the tree. They also put an angel on the top.

And the next day Ethel and Larry and Maria saw it.

You may try to imagine how they felt, but of course you cannot come close to it. Yes, they felt that, more than anything they or you or anyone could imagine.

Someone cared about Curtis. Some friend, or friends, probably. Who else? It had to be them.

They left a note thanking them, and called them the Christmas Angels.

A month later the decorations were down. A year later they were up just as Ethel and Larry and Maria had hoped. And the next year, and the next. For ten years they were always there. More notes thanking the Christmas Angels, but no reply.

Meanwhile the tree grew and Dan and Chris could no longer reach the top. One got on the shoulders of the other for a couple of years, but then even that was not enough.

And after some years went by both brought their new wives along, and then their new children. And it became a tradition.

And they knew nothing.

But something else happened. While they could not reach the top, some-how, mysteriously, an angel appeared on the tree at the very highest point.

That continued for several years.

And then Larry developed Alzheimer's and Ethel sat with him in the care home and it was Christmas. There was one wish she had.

Could Larry meet the Christmas Angels?

Maria went into dedicated internet-Facebook-Twitter overdrive and through some old high school friends presto, after a decade of not know-ing, she found the Angels.

"Is that who the tree is for?" they said.

"Yes, and you made it beautiful," said Maria.

Dan and Chris decorated a small tree outside Larry's window. Although he could not speak he said, "Thank you."

Who put the angel on the top?

???

The End

THE MAP

George Challenger was twenty when he saw the mountains across Burrard Inlet.

"Big," he said. "Those are really big."

There were no mountains in England. Coming to BC in 1896, he planned on prospecting for gold, in those same mountains. And over the following fifty years he followed the streams looking for yellow stones, and he climbed the mountains cutting the trees, and he hiked through the valleys surveying for roads and tracks and towns that were emerging.

In short, George lived the life of a tough, refined mountain man. Saying he loved this land is whispering where a storm would be more truthful.

And then he retired, and what do you do with your spare time?

"I think I'll go out to the workshop and make a little map of the province," he told his wife.

There is nothing like understating what you plan.

What George planned was colossal. Gigantic. Bigger than not only a bread basket, but a map bigger than anything that had ever been done before in the history of the world.

That is no small thing.

He used his jigsaw and cut a topographic base of Grouse Mountain out

The massive Challenger Relief Map covers more than 6,000 square feet and was entirely hand painted.

City of Vancouver Archives, AM281-S8-: CVA 180-5609-: CVA 180-5609.3

of wood. Then he cut the next layer, and the next, and you get the idea. All to scale, he cut out and constructed one mountain and then the next and the next.

With help from his wife and son he cut out three dimensional mountains from Burrard Inlet to the Yukon. From west of Atlin to east of Fort Nelson. Have you even been there?

Then he went down to Stewart, which had a glacier when he did his little project, but the warming of the air has mostly made that disappear.

152

And right across the road in the US state of Alaska, you could see Hyder. The only way in is through Stewart, BC. Kind of like Point Roberts, but not at all like that.

Point Roberts has border guards. Hyder has a sign saying if you enter or leave on this road you must report to the nearest border control office— which is in Prince Rupert, three hundred kms away.

Life is different in the north.

And then George included Masset and Sandspit and Wells Grey and back over to Bella Coola. I was once treed by a grizzly bear in Bella Coola. Luckily the tree was too skinny for the bear to climb and too strong for it to knock down or I would have had to test my reincarnation ability again. And you never know if things like that will work more than once.

And George went on to Cache Creek, where visiting reporters always try to fry an egg on the street in the middle of summer. And of course that works. It's hot. And of course that is why some people think some things on the news are dumb. A thermometer works better than an egg and doesn't waste food.

And then down to Mica Creek, and Golden, and 100 Mile House. You know where 100 Mile House is, right? One hundred miles north of where?

No. Not Vancouver. It is more than 280 miles, or 456 kms for the new way of talking, north of the big city.

It is one hundred miles north of Lillooet. Now you know where that is, right? In the 1860s it was the largest city west of Chicago and north of San Francisco.

Of course, Barkerville and Trail also each held that title for a while. That was when the mostly American gold miners were moving up and ripping up the streams and rivers and hillsides.

Lillooet was where the stage left for the gold fields more to the north and 100 Mile House was one of the stops along the rocky, bumpy, dusty, endless way, where the very tired and hungry and bladder-aching passengers could get out and ease their pains.

All the towns were mapped by George, each with a name plate, and one also appeared at the bases of the mountains or the valleys.

If you saw the map you did not need a geography course. And you got the one thing that George wanted to give you: Pride. Pride in BC.

His little retirement project went on for seven years. "Just going out to the workshop again, dear. Be back for dinner. Next month." She didn't think it was all that funny.

He started his little project in 1947. The calendar said 1954 when he put in the final piece. One little woodworking handiwork.

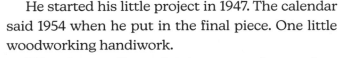

When it was all together it measured more than 6,000 square feet. Look across the street to your neighbour's house if you can. Then pretend you can see through it to the backyard. Now go to the back of their backyard.

One map.

It was 80 feet by 76 feet.

The quarter-inch fir plywood was donated by MacMillan Bloedel, but it still cost George a bundle, an estimated quarter million dollars.

It was judged by Guinness to be the largest relief map in the world.

And George gave it away. He told officials at the Pacific National Exhibition that they could have it. They owed him nothing.

The PNE had a giant building that was used for showing off BC products and produce and industry and innovation. But they did not have anything like this.

Yes, of course, they said, and they put it on a floor and over it they built a moving people carrier that stretched from Vancouver Island to the Rocky Mountains, and it moved slowly over this land that is our land to share BC with those who were here in the beginning and those who had just arrived.

"Look, there's Salmon Arm. I didn't know it was there."

"Hey, did you know there is a Dog Creek?"

"Look. I've been to Hope. And I've even gone beyond Hope. Ha, ha."

It was the single most major attraction at the fair for forty-three years. And it was free.

And then things changed. Some people were tired of the PNE taking up so much room and they wanted it gone. Others said it was the heart of the city.

There was a compromise. In 1997 the map was removed and the BC Pavilion was demolished, along with a row of other buildings. A park was put in and it was designed to look like how the area looked before the axes arrived. It is a beautiful park with ponds and streams and fishing and woodland.

Sadly, very few people go there. It has an iron fence along Hastings Street to keep it safe and most people say, "I'm not going all the way to the PNE just to go to a park."

If you happen to go, you will love it.

But meanwhile the map was taken away and since there was no available vacant sixteen-bedroom home to put it in it was stored in an Air Canada hangar at the airport.

And there it has stayed, except for a time during the Olympics in 2010 when the RCMP borrowed the Lower Mainland section and put it in their headquarters building in Richmond. It was used by the temporary army of incoming Mounties so they would know the area they were dealing with. It was the best source material they had, officials said.

Then the Olympics ended and the map went back to the hangar, and it is still there.

Late breaking news: it is now going back to the PNE. A brief story on TV about the map led to a group of activists figuring out a way to get it polished up and back home.

The map will be housed in one of the barns, which will be refurbished, and it will stretch wall to wall. It will be one of the barns where the Japanese were imprisoned during World War II.

The map, and its home, will show visitors both the magnificence and the tears of BC.

LONESOME LAKE

All Ralph Edwards wanted was to be by himself in the wilderness. He wanted to build his own home, plant and hunt his food, and even, if possible, because he was a self-taught engineer, make his own electricity.

And once he was in the wilderness he wanted to do one thing more: save some birds from starvation. That was a simple, kindly goal.

Then in 1956 *Reader's Digest* sent a world-famous writer to spend two weeks with him and the story was read by millions.

And a best-selling book was written about him.

And *National Geographic* did a spread on him.

And a movie was made about him.

And a big-time TV show did a special on him.

And all the stories talked about how he wanted to be by himself in the wilderness, with the added chapter about how he saved the birds.

The fame did not change Ralph Edwards. He went back to his home-made home by the lake and lived quietly there, feeding the birds.

Now the brief version of the story of this incredible person.

He was born in the mountains of North Carolina in 1891, or a year earlier. In places far from cities official records were low on the list of necessities.

How his parents became medical missionaries is a mystery—you don't

156

often hear of that in the wilderness, but they did—and by the time Ralph was eight, or maybe nine, he was living with them at the foothills of the Himalayas in India treating the sick.

He did not have boring parents.

Then they moved to Oregon. Okay, he got to see the world.

And by his mid-teens he was working on a railroad construction gang in British Columbia and he heard that the government wanted people to populate the north so they were giving away homesteads of 160 acres to anyone who would settle it.

There were requirements like building a home and cultivating the land, but most of all surviving was number one.

Still, he had to prove he knew about farming and building so he got some books on the subjects and read them. He was seventeen. Then he got a job on a farm and learned first hand.

By the time he was twenty-one, which was the minimum age for homesteading, he had received a 160-acre tract in the Atnarko Valley, located inland from Bella Coola on the other side of the Coast Mountains.

Try to find that with your Google Map.

He first got to Bella Coola by boat. That's a starting point for you. But he did something scary there. He started walking, sort of east, sort of south. And he kept walking for two days, forty miles, He walked through a forest that no one not born there had ever walked through.

In the woods lived grizzly bears, cougars, bobcats. There were no trails, no markers, no corner stores.

And on the edge of a lake he named Lonesome he cut trees and built a home, a multi-storey home. He gave the homestead a name: The Birches.

157

He lived there ten years, by himself, doing just what he wanted in the way he wanted.

In that time he took one break. In newspapers he got on very occasional trips to Bella Coola he learned there was a war in Europe. He closed up his home, put his garden to bed walked back to town, took a boat south and tried to join the Canadian army, but was rejected because of bad sight. So he crossed the border and joined the American army.

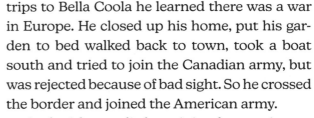

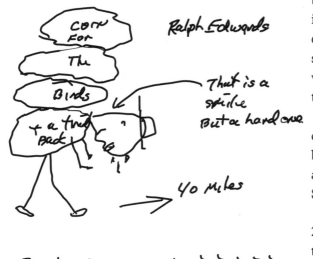

And with very little training he was in one of the most ferocious, vicious and unforgiving battles of the war, Château-Thierry. This was also the first battle where American Buffalo Soldiers were allowed to fight. They were Black.

The Germans attacked May 31, 1918. By July 22 the Germans had more than 5,000 casualties and the US a little more than 2,000. That is the simplest way of describing the carnage and showing the score card.

After the war Ralph went home. All in all a fairly normal life, and he met a woman, Ethel Hober, a local and someone who was not afraid of living a century in the past.

And then big things happened.

First, he discovered that some trumpeter swans on the lake were starving. The swans were dropping in population everywhere because of overhunting. A gaggle arrived one winter on Lonesome Lake. This was good, and bad. They were safe, but there was no food.

Ralph hiked back to Bella Coola and hauled sacks of dried corn on his back and returned to the lake. That was fine for one trip. But they were hungry again.

He walked back to town, bought a pack horse and loaded up enough

158

corn to last a few weeks. He started thinking that if he flew an airplane with the food it would be easier. So he read some books and started to build his own airplane.

And then, at age sixty-five, he went to Vancouver and got a pilot's licence—at the time he was the oldest person in Canada to do so. But he had to buy a used floatplane because the government would not allow him to fly one he made himself.

So he had an airplane, and he was feeding the geese.

You can't keep news like that quiet. The government in Ottawa hired Ralph to feed the swans, which meant he would no longer pay for the corn himself.

As for that good news travelling far, well, first *Reader's Digest,* which was one of the most read magazines in America, hired a Pulitzer Prize–winning journalist named Leland Stowe to do a little story on Ralph.

Stowe spent almost two weeks with him and was so impressed by Ralph's self-sufficiency that he also wrote a book: *Crusoe of Lonesome Lake.*

To give it to you in brief, Ralph was famous, although he did not want to be. *National Geographic* sent a photographer and did a story. In 1957 a major US TV show called *This Is Your Life* did its biggest show of the year, on Christmas Day, about Ralph.

And when everyone left he was still a good and simple fellow, who simply did what he said anyone else could do.

By the time I got there Ralph had passed away and the homestead was run by his daughter, Trudy. She showed me the water-powered sawmill and the electric generator powered by a river.

But the most ingenious idea was the hangar for his floatplane. It was big. "How did he build that?" I asked.

"Well," she said, "in the winter when the lake was frozen he piled up snow on the ice. It was three times higher than he could reach. Then he shaped it into what he wanted the hanger to be. Then he climbed on the snow and starting at the top built the hangar."

She looked so proud of him. "In the spring when the snow melted there was his hangar."

Sadly much later a forest fire destroyed all that Ralph had built and the land reverted back to the province. Today it is part of Tweedsmuir Provincial Park.

Just one little more adventure. I was there with a young cameraman from Hong Kong, Ken Chu. He was very good with a camera but his wilderness techniques were limited to high-rise apartments and a concrete city.

We had flown to the Edwards home by floatplane and landed on the lake, then took a long walk to their cabin.

On the way back we were gone about a quarter hour when the bush pilot who got us there said, "Uh oh!" Those were his exact words.

They were followed by, "There's a grizzly down there." He pointed to a valley. "Looks like a mother with two cubs."

That was followed by, "This is bad."

And that was followed by, "Get up a tree, quick."

I said to Ken, "Take a picture."

Despite the bears Ralph Edwards made his life an adventure, which is what many dream of. And the swans that he saved have flourished and are still there.

ADANAC

Opposite:
In an effort to clean up its reputation, residents petitioned to have the east portion of Union Street renamed Adanac Street. "Adanac" was once such a common name for streets, boats and businesses few paused to consider its origin.
Art Grice and F 11 Photographics photo, City of Vancouver Archives, AM336-S3-2-: CVA 677-921

She just could not stand living there. Oh, her home was wonderful. The garden beautiful. The neighbours friendly. "But I hate to tell anyone where I live," she said.

She was Mary Ann Galbraith, born near the end of the 1800s into a Vancouver that was growing like a teenager, with pimples.

Some things were exciting and wonderful. The new streetcars that could take you to English Bay. What a wonderful excursion that was done in less than a day.

On the other hand there were the bad things: criminals, gamblers and ladies of the night. And many of them were on Union Street in East Vancouver. And Mary lived on Union Street.

"What happens when I tell anyone where I live? They turn around, that's what happens," she said.

But she did not live on the bad part of Union, no sir, she lived on the good part of Union, which was east of Vernon Street. Look on a map, it will help.

No, there was no gambling and drinking on her side, but still, that name. It ruined her days.

She campaigned and wrote letters and begged for SOMETHING to be done.

Mary was also active in local politics and volunteered as an election scrutineer. Surely that would carry some weight. And it did. Deep in a back office in the old city hall building at Main and Hastings someone said, "We should help."

How often do you hear that from a city hall official?

"But we can't throw out those people on Union Street."

"Those people" were the ones Mary did not like.

They thought and thought and Eureka!

"I have an idea," said a bright government employee. "If we can't change the world we can change what the world is called."

That was brilliance. What is in a name? EVERY-THING.

"Mary does not like living on Union Street. We cannot ask her to move. And we cannot get rid of those neighbours on Union Street who she does not like. But we *can* make where she is sound like a different place.

So much of life, maybe everything, is in a name. I may have already told you about the terrible fate of the rapeseed, but I will again. Now there was a scientifically bad choice of a brand to put on a pretty flower.

It is yellow and grows wild across much of the middle of Canada. And if you press its seeds you get a smooth, clear, mild-flavoured oil, with an awful name.

For, well, forever, it was used to squirt on machinery, which worked well. The machines worked and folks would crudely joke, squirt some rape on that and it will be okay.

So ugly. So much, thankfully, in the past, I hope.

But then someone working in a marketing company far from a farm or machines had an idea. Those wonderful things from nowhere that change everything.

"This stuff is great, it just needs a new name. And I have it," he said. He had just been to the supermarket and bought some Mazola oil to do his frying. What is Mazola? he thought. It's a brilliant combination of corn and oil. And it sells like hot cakes.

He tried different combinations and words and presto: "canola," a marriage of "Canada" and "oil."

I never met him, but I hope he got a raise.

And soon canola was on grocery shelves that rapeseed never touched. Canola is now the second largest selling cooking oil in the world, after olive. Not a bad comeback after a knockout.

Now back to Mary: "Do something," she said. "I don't know what, just do something."

Then the good thing. That person in the small office in city hall said, "Change the name."

"Of what?" someone must have said.

"Of her street, of course."

Now began the harder part. "To what?"

That was an all-nighter. Can't have flowers, we don't do flowers. Can't have trees, they are up on Broadway.

One name was proposed: Barnard, after Francis Stillman Barnard who was on the Vancouver Improvement Committee. He fought against the CPR taking so much land and folks liked him and said he should have a street in his name.

But then they said Barnard is almost like Burrard and the mail will never get delivered. And then as it was 1918 and the big ugly war was over an alderman said to call it Victory Street. But it was crossing Victoria Drive and who would know where they were if they met at Victoria and Victory?

I tell you this only because this is what really goes on in city halls, around the world.

And then, inspiration. Someone, unnamed, said Mary loves this country, right?

Yes.

"We can't call it Canada Street, but what about if we change the letters around and give it a new sound, ADANAC?"

"Sold! Brilliant. Done. Now let's get on with raising taxes."

And so Mary no longer lived on Union Street. And over the next sixty years she had nine children and she and her husband lived peacefully on a street with a pure reputation, not like those who lived on the other side of Vernon Street, which was called Union Street and was the same street where Mary lived.

PS: There is a wonderful local brewery now on Adanac, with people drinking beer.

PPS: Adanac turns back into Union as soon as it crosses into Burnaby.

PPPS: Union Street is now one of the trendiest, most sought after streets in the city.

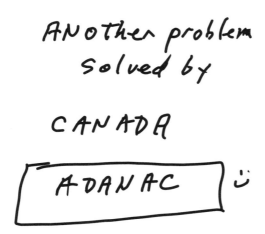

JOHN MORTON

Y^{ou} simply can not imagine what it looked like. I can because I was
there, but you can't.

The forest beginning at the edge of the water in what is now Coal
Harbour—where the Bayshore takes in famous visitors, including Howard
Hughes, who boarded up the windows so no one could see in and he could
not see out—and Brockton Point in Stanley Park—where the lighthouse
replaced the fellow throwing dynamite over the water to tell the fishermen
it was six o'clock—was once a forest like none other that had ever existed.

Sorry, every time I mention anywhere in the city it reminds me of something else that was there. That is the problem with living through it all and
not dying and every place being my old neighbourhood.

You know your old neighbourhood and the skateboard accidents you
had and the games you played? Of course you do.

Everywhere is that way for me.

And there was Coal Harbour and the crazy guy named John Morton.

He came here in 1862. That was so early I was still in the army and was
clearing land to make Kingsway and North Road and trying to sneak home
at night to my beautiful wife.

But there was John—and two others, his cousin Sam Brighouse and a friend Bill Hailstone. In short, after they left the settlement of New Westminster and went north and then west there was nothing there, except trees, and bears and no place to sleep. The Bayshore was not quite ready for guests.

They were not loggers. They had no money. They could not run a sawmill. They could not fish. What in the world are you doing here? I thought that later when I heard about them.

John was a potter. Oh, good. That will do you well, where plates were not available for most meals. Cups were made of tin and bowls were your cups when they were empty of the beer, which was a good business to be in.

William Hailstone, Sam Brighouse and John Morton were nicknamed the Three Greenhorns for shelling out $550 for land in Vancouver's West End that is now worth billions.

J.D. Hall photo, City of Vancouver Archives, AM54-S4-: Port P775

They were adventurers. What does that mean? Well, they heard about this place far away with forests and gold and something else: opportunity.

Again, what does that mean?

"I knew I could do something there," John said to me when I met him years later. "I did not know what it was, but there was opportunity to do something if I could figure out what it was."

Now there was a fellow I admired. He had courage. If he was homeless, sorry for bringing that up, but if he was he would start cleaning up the debris at the tent cities and charging the city a dollar a pound for everything.

And if they said that was a city job and he was taking employment away from city workers he would clean and adjust tents for residents at a minimal charge. And if they would not pay he would move out and open his own private campground and plant grass and have rules for tenants. Don't laugh. He would have.

Instead, his trio walked, yes walked, from New West to as far as they could go and stopped at the water, Burrard Inlet. Then they turned left and walked. And after 60,000 steps or more, they were in good shape, and they found coal.

It was not gold, but it was sticking right out of the shore, right about where Cardero's Restaurant is now, and John said, "It's black, but it's gold." But sadly he knew, because he knew such things, that it was not good coal for burning. On the other hand, where there was coal there was also good earth for making pottery. So he found gold. His gold.

Later I asked, "So, what's the big deal?"

"These wonderful people will soon build homes here. And they will have wives and wives will want dishes and bowls. There is no bigger deal than a wife."

168

There in front of me was a genius.

Then John and his cousin and friend did something really stupid. Have you ever bought a time share that you were told had great ocean views and would attract the upper crust of buyers, and location, location, etc.? And you got a great breakfast.

John and the others were told about a hunk of land not too far from the coal that might be worth something, someday, if the stars and plants and earthworms all aligned at the same moment on the hand-set clock.

It had no name. It was "over there, see, there," said the dealer, who pointed sort of south and sort of west and then dropped his finger.

"How much?" asked John.

"For you, and only you, $550."

That was ten years' pay for any job below King.

"You stake your claim. I'll do the paperwork and you move it," said the man with the big smile and friendly wave—and the sausage muffin in his hand ready for the next victim, sorry, investor.

"You idiots!" said the understanding fellows in the bar in New West. The news was everywhere when they got back home to their hotel. "You are nuts. You're out of your minds. Do you know what you have done?"

They were called Greenhorns, the Three Greenhorns. They knew nothing about anything and making fun of them was sport.

Poor John. I was there that night having just one beer before going home to Mary. He looked so sheepish, if that is a look. He was embarrassed. Obviously, these guys knew more about life than he did. They were big and strong, he was not, they were wise, look at their furrowed brows, he was not.

"Ha, ha, ha," they said.

I bought him a beer.

"Why'd you buy that land?" I asked.

"Looked like a good deal," he said.

"You think anyone is going to leave here to go there?" I asked.

He sipped. "This is pretty good," he said.

"Craft beer made by local folks," I said. "Made with the finest water where beavers poop and fish have sex," I said.

"My hope is when the forests are cut down people will move to the seashore," he said.

"It'll never happen," I said. "There are too many trees and not enough people. But good luck."

I may be immortal, but BOY, CAN I BE WRONG!

In less time than I lived another lifetime, the West End became the most densely packed area of the city and homes on top of homes going up to the sky were selling for more per square inch than John paid per acre, and they were multiplied on each floor, and if you wanted to go somewhere to get away from real estate agents or time share pushers you could go to the beach at English Bay.

And John was worth a billion, no billions upon billions, when he died. But most of all, before he died people had a lot of kind and admiring and envious words for him, and no one ever again said he was foolish. In truth, he was smarter, and braver, than all of us.

ROBERT BURNABY

Some people are just plain good at schmoozing. It is an art.

If there is someone important to know the schmoozer will put a frame around him or her and admire the subject.

The schmoozer enters a room with the eye of an eagle, picks out the one with the plumpest reputation, the finest clothing, and the one surrounded by the most admirers.

And then he will schmooze. It is a talent sharpened at every encounter.

Enter Robert Burnaby. He was born not to do any actual work, those around him said, but to work on those who were in charge of those who worked.

He was handsome, debonair and well dressed. His father was a church minister, which set him in good company, but not the highest.

He became a civil servant in London and set his aim at flattering the biggest of the big wigs. Out of that came a letter of recommendation from one of the top wigs. That was more valuable than gold because gold can be cashed in only once.

When he heard the news about BC—this was 1858, and the Queen had just declared it a colony—and about the gold there, he saw opportunity, not for gold but for rubbing elbows, and he was on the next non-stop boat with his letter.

First stop was Victoria, which he loved. This was a true English town, but the fellow in charge, Big James Douglas, was not the type to be flattered. And he did not need another outsider to deal with. He was already having trouble with that Colonel Moody, who got here after Douglas had done all the legwork, and that was a big enough problem.

On the other hand Burnaby thought Moody was the perfect elbow to rub. He was powerful and probably needed someone to make suggestions. Trouble was New Westminster was not civilized. It was dirty and rough, but never turn down opportunity.

With his letter he was hired by Moody as his private secretary, which meant he got the inside scoop on the big and small events. His first task was to survey the big lake Moody had heard about, which would supply water for the new capital.

With us Sappers carrying his equipment and doing the surveying and leading the way, Burnaby headed into the forest to the northwest and came back with a map, which we drew, of the location of fresh water.

After he showed it to Colonel Moody the map had one big addition: written at the top was *Burnaby Lake*.

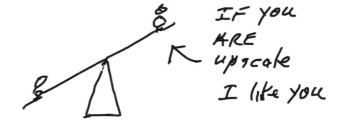

So humble.

His next task was to take a walk on Kingsway, which we Sappers were still building, to Gastown and then go west to investigate rumours of coal at the edge of the water.

With us Sappers again doing the carrying and leading, Burnaby got to what is now Coal Harbour and said, "By golly, there *is* coal here. It would be good for a person to own this." It was government business, but Burnaby had no trouble mixing that with his personal goals.

However, there were three gentlemen who already owned it. They were

173

John Morton and his two friends, who you just met. They had staked it, bought it and paid for it, and had an official government document to prove it.

"No problem," said Burnaby. "Because you see I filed a claim BEFORE they filed a claim."

When we returned to New West he went into a back room of his office and after a goodly long time he came out with a piece of paper. "I finally found it," he said. "Here's my prior claim to the harbour and 128 acres around it."

You can imagine how John Morton said, "Of course. Sorry. You are right."

No. We can't imagine that either. Morton said, "I'm taking you to court," and there Judge Chartres Brew examined Burnaby's document and said, officially for the record: "This claim was obviously written by a liar or a knave."

"Knave" was a bad thing to be called back then. It was disparagingly applied to persons considered base, dishonest or worthless.

It was not good for Burnaby's reputation. So he

Robert Burnaby is a leading contender for the title of having the most things named after him for the least reason of any BC pioneer.

Harbour Publishing Archives

left New West and moved to Victoria, where he thought he had the qualifications for politics. He was elected to the Legislative Assembly, one term, and surrounded himself with the biggest names in the province.

He did good things, helping create the Chamber of Commerce and serving as president of the Amateur Dramatic Association of Victoria. And he helped establish the first Masonic Lodge in BC.

And then, before returning to England in 1874, after retiring due to health issues, he sold the city thirteen acres of land near Ross Road that the city wanted to use as a cemetery. How in the world could he have known they wanted that land before he bought it?

In the end you could ask what did Robert Burnaby do to get a city, a mountain, a park, a street in Vancouver, an island and a narrows in Haida Gwaii, in total eleven places, named after him?

Well, some say it is not what you do that counts as much as who you know. That is sad. But for some, apparently, it's true.

ABE and MORRIS

He started with an old and rusty child's wagon. He went up and down the back alleys looking for anything that might be worth something in someone else's eyes. He had already been through Hell. In comparison, the back alleys of Vancouver were not so bad.

It was 1949 and four years before that Abe Miedzygorski was in a concentration camp in Poland. There was a long number tattooed on his left forearm. His crime in the eyes of some was of course that he was Jewish.

Now step out of Hell. Because of luck, because of the way the stars are, because of things neither he nor really anyone know about, he ended up in Canada, and later in Vancouver. He was lost, alone and needed to work.

So he found a wagon, and that began Abe's Junk Shop. It was next door to Morris's Junk Shop, which was on the corner of Main and Twenty-eighth. Morris also had a number on his arm, but he was different.

I could have gone to Abe's shop every day just for the relief from everything else. Abe was behind the counter with a round, red face and white beard.

Nearby, always nearby, was Goldie, his wife, also with a number on her arm.

One would laugh, then the other would laugh. Abe would say, "Goldie, you are today my sweetheart and tomorrow."

176

And Goldie would laugh, "What about yesterday? Didn't yesterday count for anything?"

"Yesterday was good. Today is better."

It really did not matter what either said, the other enjoyed the words like pieces of chocolate, one leading to another.

I would go in and ask if he had something new, meaning old, that I could do a story about and Abe would say, "You have come to the right place. How about this picture in a nice frame. It is an authentically old picture of a famous old person."

"Who?"

"It is a mysterious old person who was famous for not telling his name, but it is genuinely old."

And then he would show me a Coca-Cola sign that had beautiful rust and nicks and dents.

"You don't find signs like this just anywhere." And then he would laugh.

Junk was Abe's gold mine, even if the gold vein was as thin as thread. He knew junk and he knew how to laugh and after having life taken from him he and Goldie were putting it back with each breath and each word.

Morris was different. He too had lost everything, but then he lost something more than everything. He lost his laughter.

Morris kept collecting junk, but he would not part with it. Every shelf, every bit of floor space was filled with things. If you squeezed into his shop and picked up a lamp and asked how much it cost Morris would take it from you, look at it, and then say, "This is not for sale."

"Well what about this?" you would say as you picked up a toaster.

He would take it again, turn it over in his hands, and say again, "This is not for sale."

You could go through everything and in the end nothing was for sale. Morris could not bear to part with anything.

I never figured out how he made any money, but somehow he did. But sadly, over the years I tried to talk to him he never responded with anything other than a grunt to my hello. And there the conversation died.

Next door was laughter and warmth and excitement, with each new old thing Abe had for sale.

A classic moment for me, maybe for him, came after he retired and the shop was taken over by his son Sid, who changed the word on the front of the shop—from Junk to Antiques.

Abe was watching the shop one day while his son was out. He leaned in the open doorway with his arms folded. You could still see a few of the numbers where his sleeve was pulled up.

He was slowly shaking his head as I walked up.

"What's wrong?"

With a Yiddish accent that was musical he said, "Mine son. I don't know what's wrong with him. Junk was good enough for me. Junk bought him food all his life. Junk paid for his schooling."

He looked up at the new sign on his old shop. "Now he is too good for junk."

Then he laughed, loudly, a laugh that showed he understood that no matter how much the world changes you can survive anything.

Abe and Morris. Forget your self help books and your TV psychologists. Just think of Abe and Morris. All the answers are there.

JACK WASSERMAN

It is not often people fear a reporter, unless you were Richard Nixon and you had a couple of guys like Woodward and Bernstein after you. Or if you were Donald Trump and had CNN and the *New York Times* doing the same.

But in the somewhat quiet and laid back Vancouver of the 1950s and '60s there was just one, and everyone who might be doing something they did not want others to know about was terrified he might see them.

If Jack Wasserman, with his sharply cut face and his cigarette and his well-fitting suit, walked in to a dark smoked-filled club, hands that were holding hands would be dropped and dancers who were snuggling dancers would suddenly be dancing by themselves.

Jack was not a news reporter, although what he reported on was hotter news than what was on page one.

"Did you read Wasserman today?"

"I couldn't believe it. That guy, you know that guy who's so big in the market, was with someone who was not his wife."

"I know. He is going to be in deep do-do."

Jack Wasserman was a gossip reporter, and what is better to read about than someone's success? It is someone's downfall. It is a terrible thing to say, but true. The *Times* of London is accurate and fair, but the British tabloids sell more papers.

Wasserman would report on things he heard, or that others overhead somewhere, usually behind a curtain. The name of the person he was writing about would be in bold type and then... that person might just have been with another person who they were not normally with.

To sue him you would have to go to court and demand that he prove what he had written. The problem with that was you *were* with that person, and others saw you. So you said nothing, publicly, and just did your talking and denying at home.

The hottest club was the Cave. It lasted forty years, looking like, of course, a cave right from caveman days. There were stalactites made of burlap and plaster hanging from the ceiling and the walls looked like the walls of a rock-bound world where dark and exciting things could happen.

The first thing you did after sitting down was order a bottle of ginger ale or 7-Up and a pitcher of ice. That is a sobering thought. And then you would sneak a bottle of whiskey out of your pocket or purse and fill the glasses, with just a little ice and pop added to hide your sins

In most clubs there were metal sleeves under the tables into which you could slide your bottle. Otherwise, back in your pocket or purse. This was all done while you were wearing a neat suit and tie and your companion had a sparkling new dress bought just for the evening. It was embarrassing to be a sneak when you look so chic, but it was always followed by laughter.

Ha, we did not get caught, again.

And when the police came in, which they often did, all the bottles went into hiding in the usual places. The police would pass between the tables looking and looking and seeing nothing.

Jack Wasserman
made it big in the
best way, by haunting
the bars and night
clubs of Vancouver's
entertainment district,
later designated
"Wasserman's Beat."
Croton Studio photo,
Vancouver Public Library
80377

On the way out they might be handed an envelope with some papers inside, although no one ever saw this either.

Sometimes, though, there were raids where bottles were seen and confiscated, much to everyone's surprise. "I have no idea how that got there, constable. Honest."

One night thirty bottles came out of the Panorama Roof, which was the most prestigious of the clubs. It was on the roof of the Hotel Vancouver, where the best of the best would go.

"Honest, I never saw this illegal bottle before you discovered it under the table in front of me. It must have been left by someone else."

Why some nights were like this, who knew? Maybe no envelopes were received the night before—but that is only a bit of gossip, which is the intoxicant Jack Wasserman dealt in.

In addition to the hand holding and the ginger ale, many of the biggest names in entertainment were appearing at the clubs: Louis Armstrong, Oscar Peterson, Lenny Bruce, Diana Ross and the Supremes, and Lena Horne. They brought the crowds Wasserman wrote about.

There was just one problem with having those dark and smoky places as your beat, night after night and years leading into years. He did not get danger pay. He did not have an oxygen mask. And he smoked, as did nearly everyone he saw and wrote about.

On the night of April 6, 1977, while giving a speech at the Hotel Vancouver during a roast of Gordon Gibson, a famous politician, Wasserman made a joke and leaned forward, banging his head on the microphone.

Everyone laughed. That was funny.

It was not funny. He was dead. Heart attack at fifty.

Hornby Street, for a few blocks out front of where the Cave was, has been named by the city as Jack Wasserman's Beat.

No club, no whiskey, no gossip, not much smoking. And sadly, for the people who go to pubs in blue jeans, who was Jack Wasserman?

JACK WEBSTER

T his Jack also smoked, even when he was on the air, although for the sake of the boss he tried to hide his ashtray. Still you could see the slipstream of white smoke rising as he was getting more and more adamant on whatever subject he was adamant about today.

In short, Jack Webster could do no wrong. He was not feared, unless you were a politician who he disagreed with. He was loved by most, almost all... okay, everyone except those who would get a reprimand: "Stupid, stupid, stupid!"

That was a poke in the eye from the old guy with the Scottish accent.

Jack left school at fourteen because he wanted to work at a newspaper. Whatever he could learn behind a desk with a teacher at the front of the room would be time that he was not learning first hand at a fire or crime scene or rally for some outlandish politician. You learn a lot in those late-night classrooms on the street.

And he ate it up with an appetite that could not be satisfied. The only time he was away from news was during World War II when he rose to the rank of major in the British army. And unlike some other officers, he never once mentioned his rank after the war.

But he did go into battle. First at the *Vancouver Sun*, where he covered

labour stories, but then into radio where his voice and attitude and ferocious attacks on what he saw as wrongdoings got him the biggest audience this city had ever heard.

Within ten years of arriving in Vancouver in 1947 he was making $100,000 a year, which was more than the prime minister, premier or basically anyone else, outside of some criminals.

He covered the courts like no one else because he had one tool that in the reporting trade was so smart to get, and so rare. On his own he studied shorthand, the basic skill of every secretary who has had to listen to their boss muttering idiocy and turn it into a polite business letter.

Only women knew shorthand. Only women, and Webster.

In court no cameras were allowed, and sadly they still are not. No recording machines. Only a pen and a notebook, and reporters would take notes, some of them legible.

As a lifelong note taker I have to admit that I look at things I have written and have no idea what I wrote. It was important at that moment, it was immediate, it was something that I did not want to forget—and then I look at it later and it is a scribble, done by a five-year-old.

Not Webster. He went into court with his stenographer's notebook,

Scottish immigrant Jack Webster used his aggressive reporting style to rise to the top of BC journalism, embracing print, radio then television.
Croton Studio photo, Vancouver Public Library 79214

the kind that folded over at the top, while the other reporters would have sheets of newsprint that they folded into thirds and put in their breast pocket. That was tradition. That was also stupid, stupid, stupid.

After court Webster could transcribe word for word what was said to his typewriter and have a solid story for the newspaper. The other reporters, even the good ones, would spread out their papers and try to figure out which one was first and which after that. And then they would read, "He said he didn't have no gun when the killing happened."

Who said that, the witness or the accused? It must have been, darn, I wish I had said who said what they said.

Not Webster.

When he went to radio in 1953 after a nasty dispute with the *Vancouver Sun* he became famous. The gruff Scotsman was the people's friend.

During a riot at the BC Pen the prisoners wanted to talk to Webster. There was no negotiating with prison officials or frightened people from the government. That was useless. It was only Webster the prisoners could trust.

He was there before the sun set. Prisons are terrible places. They are not meant to be nice, but the old prisons were worse than terrible.

The stink, the fires, the smoke from burning piles of stinking blankets, and the noise, that was the worst, the noise of screams and banging and hollers, not shouts, hollers, bouncing off the hard walls that made your brain curl up for safety inside your skull.

And in this world would be negotiations, with Webster in the middle. The prisoners got some of what they wanted, which was simply slightly better treatment, and Webster got more fame, which he earned.

But later, in the quiet of a courtroom in the building that is now the art gallery, came his biggest reporting success, and all because of shorthand.

It was a hearing, not even a trial. It was a hearing to see if there was enough evidence to have a trial, but the accused was Walter Mulligan, the chief constable of Vancouver. He was a tough cop, big, six foot two and 230 pounds. That's big, and everyone wants a big, tough cop to be on your side.

Except Mulligan was accused of taking bribes and kickbacks and dealing with bookies and criminals in general, anyone so long as they would slide some cash over to him.

He was exposed by two local reporters, not Webster, just two low-level beat reporters who stood in the rain to get their stories. They knew what was going on, but their papers would not print their stories.

"No kid, that's the police chief you are talking about. We are not putting that in our paper." So they went over the heads of their editors and gave the story to a newspaper in Toronto, where Mulligan was not the chief of police. The paper printed an extra 10,000 copies to be shipped to the streets of Vancouver.

An inquiry was ordered. Whoever heard of such a thing, the police chief accused of such behaviour? That was silly, the public said. Then two of Chief Mulligan's detectives took out their pistols and shot themselves in their heads in the squad room on the second floor of the police station at 312 Main Street.

In court came the accusations and the defences, and every day a woman with a big, floppy hat sat in the gallery listening. She was Mulligan's mistress, for whom he had bought a large, expensive house where he could visit her occasionally for tea, as they said in testimony.

And it was that testimony that Webster recorded in his steno book. Word for word. And when he went on his show in the afternoon he started by saying, "This is a story that the *Sun* does not have."

The *Sun* reporter was still trying to read his notes. Webster was reading verbatim.

The weird thing about this hearing—actually it is not weird, it is the way the justice system works when you have enough lawyers and money, which is sad—but the weird thing was, during the legal proceedings Mulligan applied for residency in the US and it was granted.

While the lawyers were still inside the courtroom he moved to California and took a job selling flowers. Who could find anything incriminating about that?

Inside the court the judge found there were no guilty parties, and no charges were laid. Webster said it was a whitewash. He said it loudly, but the system was still more powerful than a radio commentator.

And right after the verdict Mulligan gave up his green card and came back to Canada and lived peacefully on Vancouver Island, in Oak Bay, and died quietly and honestly at eighty-five.

Webster started a new career on television when he was sixty. What time did he start? "Nine a.m. *prrre-cisely!*" It is good to have a trademark that tells people what time he will be expecting you to be waiting for him.

He died at eighty, with a giant following and the Order of Canada. And now the Jack Webster Foundation gives awards to outstanding reporters and helps those who want to become that.

Not bad for a guy who quit school and still wound up with ink-stained hands.

DON TIMBRELL

There were many Don Timbrells. Hundreds, and hundreds more. They were different sizes, ages and genders, and they had different names. But they were all Don Timbrells with the same story.

I was with Don when he returned to the orphanage, the home that replaced his after the bombs fell on London. The long barracks buildings, his home for his formative years, were in Duncan, on Vancouver Island.

It is best to let him tell the story.

"We heard the sirens, heard the airplanes and we knew what would happen. We ran for the basement."

This was ongoing. You listened to the screaming of the bombs falling, ripping apart the air as they came down. And then BOOM. And the earth shook. And dust was blown out of cracks in the bomb shelter and you were scared. You were below ground. You were safe.

This time it wasn't like that.

"My mother pushed us down the stairs to the basement and then *bang*. This wasn't a hit down the street. The explosion was right behind our heads, up there, in the kitchen."

Up there meant where his mother and father were, still up there, except he knew they would not be there at the top of the stairs that led to the basement. Now there *was no* up there. And there were no parents coming down behind Don and his brother.

The two boys were left in the rubble of the shelves of canned food that was stored downstairs. They waited, and hoped and secretly prayed, then crawled slowly up the stairs.

Their parents were dead.

The days afterwards were confused and frightening but in short they wound up on a train, then a ship that took them to Montreal. And from there a long train ride to Vancouver, and then a ferry ride. They had no idea where they were. They heard the name Canada. It meant nothing to them. They missed their parents.

For the next five years the orphanage in Duncan was their home and their mom was the woman who was called the Dorm Mother. She sat near the exit door in a chair at the end of two long rows of beds.

She was there in case someone started screaming during the night. That happened.

"What I remember the most was two things: Christmas and Sunday mornings."

"Those are different things," I mentioned.

He smiled. He had a nice smile. He was thin no matter what he ate and

During World War II, many British orphans found themselves relocated to this orphanage near Duncan, BC.

Image H-02745 courtesy of the Royal BC Museum and Archives

he wore a turtleneck shirt no matter what the fashion was. Please don't ask what meaning the turtleneck shirts have. Those who remember Don are remembering them.

"For Christmas we would be given an Eaton's catalogue in the summer and we would fight over it. We were told to pick out one thing we wanted and it could not cost more than five dollars."

We walked outside into the view of the surrounding countryside. It was nice, at least as nice as it could be considering the last time you saw your parents they were dead in a pile of blown apart wood and plaster.

Life is hard for many.

"We would fight over those catalogues. 'You've had it long enough. It's my turn.' And then we would want this cap pistol and the girls would want that doll and then we would change our minds."

And then a few days later it was Sunday.

"We would stand at attention at the foot of our beds and wait for those who might adopt us to walk by." All the kids stood still. They were told not to look at any of those who were searching for someone to take home. "If you look you will not be picked," they were told.

That was enough to keep their eyes straight ahead.

"Please pick me," Don said he wished every time someone passed by.

And then came Christmas and he had not been picked. They were told to tie one of their socks, a clean one, to the foot of their bed.

"We went to sleep early. It was dark early. We could not sleep but we did sleep and someone would get up early, some kid ten beds away, and yell, 'It's Christmas!' And everyone was up crawling to the foot of their beds."

This was the best day of the year. They each pulled open their sock and at the top was a date, a sticky, dried date wrapped in wax paper.

"Got rid of that quick," Don said. "And under it was a new pair of socks.

Everyone got socks. We threw those up on the bed. And then right below the socks, the next thing in our hand was the thing we hoped for."

His smile was the same as it was forty years earlier.

"There was the thing we picked out in the catalogue. We played with it all day. We wouldn't let it go. This was ours and it was supposed to last a year but sometimes it got ruined in a day."

Later he mentioned that below the gift was an orange. He did not remember eating it.

And on one Sunday during some year someone looked at his face, told him to open his mouth so they could see his teeth, and he heard them say, "He's OK."

They were loving parents. They had taken on problems that he did not know about. The problems were with him learning about new parents. Again, life is hard, but some do very well.

Don went on to learn photography and became one of the very early cameramen at a new TV station called BCTV. Then he became the chief cameraman. He and his wife adopted a daughter, who did well. His two sons also did well, one was a cameraman, the other an RCMP officer.

Don did well.

There were hundreds and hundreds of Dons with his same story. Life may be hard, but if you don't let it kill you, you can make it into a work of beauty.

W.P. KINSELLA

The last time I saw Bill he was staring at a row of seven wooden tiles with letters burned onto them trying to squeeze a B and an E in between two other words.

I forgot what the words were, but I asked him if it was as hard as it looked.

"Are you kidding?" he said, "Writing is hard. This is effervescent pleasure."

Bill liked words. But now his tall frame, tall and lanky even when crouched in a chair in a Scrabble tournament in the Masonic Temple on Granville Street, was bent over seven little letters. He was devising an impossible solution to an impossible combination of words on the cardboard game in front of him.

W.P. Kinsella was in love with writing and words but the writing part of it made loving hard. The words were his lovers.

He wanted to be a writer when he was five, or at least that is his story, and who would disagree? When he was older he took creative writing courses at several universities and then he went home to write.

But how do you support yourself while pounding the keys on a manual typewriter?

Pizza. That was the answer. Not eating it but making it, and then later delivering it. He opened Caesar's Pizza in Victoria in 1967, and it was a hit. He could deliver the pies at night and write during the day.

And he turned out beautiful stories of Indigenous life in Canada, which he loved learning about and reading about and weaving into stories for others. They won some awards, but not many readers, or at least not many buyers of the books.

He went on writing and delivering pizzas. And in 1972 he sold the restaurant so he could focus more on his writing, which is all he really wanted to do, even if he had only minor success.

But then something happened that changed everything in his life. It was one of those little things, a little suggestion from someone that gets passed off as an idle, supposed to be funny, comment but turned out to be a giant stone from the sky that changes everything when it hits the earth.

Years later, right after the book became a movie, I was visiting him in his apartment in White Rock, the same small couple of rooms where he worked during the day after working at night— still delivering pizza, but for someone else.

"I had this friend," he said, "who said to me one day, 'You would like to sell your books in the US, right?'"

"Well, yeah, of course," Bill said.

"'Then write something they want to read, like maybe...'" and there Bill paused. He said his friend paused. He said his friend was looking for something to suggest and obviously had nothing to suggest.

And then Bill mimicked his friend, "Then he said, 'Like maybe, maybe... (long pause) BASEBALL! Americans like baseball.'"

Bingo. The rock hit the planet.

Bill went to the White Rock Library and started reading. And there it was, right between the covers of an old book: "The Black Sox Scandal of 1919." The Chicago White Sox were accused of throwing the World Series against the Cincinnati Reds. They were paid for this.

It ruined the unshakeable faith Americans had in baseball as a game of innocence and trust. Eight players were banned for life. And among the cheating players was the best player on the team, in fact, the best player on any team. In fact, one of the best players ever to play, ever.

Shoeless Joe Jackson. He was born into total and severe poverty. He worked in a cotton mill when he was six. He never went to school.

But man, oh man, could he hit and catch and throw. There was none better. In the list of the 100 best players ever in baseball he is number 35.

Bill read the whole story without leaving the library, then checked out the book and went home, to deliver pizza, and afterwards he read the story again.

And yes, Joe did play without shoes, but just once. His new cleats gave him blisters so one day he was out on the field barefoot.

What better character to write about?

And so Bill went on delivering his pizza and writing. "It was hard, the writing, hard, as always," he said. When he was finished he had *Shoeless Joe*, a bestseller in the US. "It paid well," he said. He did not add for the first time.

The movie, *Field of Dreams* starring Kevin Costner, came from the book. And that paid well, much better than the book alone.

W.P. Kinsella—William Patrick, but no one called him that, it was either Bill or W.P.—came from Edmonton. He was raised on a homestead and did not see a school until he was eleven. That is not what is called a late start, that is out of the gate after all the other horses are halfway around the track.

By the time he finished high school he had seen one Shakespeare play and *Peter Pan*, both put on by students. But that was enough to make him want to write. And making and delivering pizzas. It paid so much that he could give up writing if he wanted to. But he didn't.

BC author W.P. "Bill" Kinsella wrote a book about baseball in a calculated attempt to attract sales in the US. The book became a classic film, *Field of Dreams*, and Bill became one of America's favourite baseball writers.

Harbour Publishing Archives

"Scrabble is fun," he said right before he put down two letters at an intersection of two long words and said, "That's," pause while he counted, "sixty-four points."

I could not even read them, much less spell them, much less come up with them. Bill loved them.

FRIENDLY FRED HUME

Here's another fellow with no schooling and no money who became an intellectual, industrial and political powerhouse—and also, of course, rich. And probably the best thing about him was he was nice. If you dug around for some dirt in his life you would have gotten dirty and tired and frustrated but you would have found nothing.

Fred Hume made me proud. He was descended from two Sapper families, which means the genes were strong and good and honest. This is where I do not talk about my family, in which the girls were good. Period.

Back to Fred. He was born in a house in New Westminster, not too unusual in 1893, and he quit school at thirteen, also not too unusual. And he did every kind of job he could find: fishing, driving horses, inside a mill, clerking in a store and up poles stringing telegraph lines.

Again, all of that was the ordinary life of a young man in the early 1900s.

Woman, sadly, had only marriage to look forward to, and having children. The world really has not been fair. But one of them, Fanny Rumble, was lucky to be the one who Fred married. They had two children when the telephone company he was climbing poles for wanted to transfer him to Victoria.

"No, sir," he said. "I'm not moving my family away from their friends and family. I quit."

Then he joined with his brother-in-law, Percy Rumble, and they opened a tiny fix-it shop repairing the newest gadgets that every woman wanted: the electric toaster and plug-in electric iron. They made life so easy, up until when they did not work.

With a couple of soldering irons and screwdrivers Fred and Percy fixed them at seventy-five cents each.

Now if you work really hard and smile and are friendly and add more hard work and do a good job with what you are doing you pretty well have the market sewn up. Their business grew into a general electrical supply and repair business that was dealing with the major hotels and other big-time companies.

Then someone suggested to Fred that he should get into politics in New West and help that city, so he did.

Immediately he ran up against those who were not friendly. It does not seem to matter where or when you go in politics or business or anything, you will run into people who are not out for the good of others.

Some of those who did not like Fred's outgoing attitude tried to get him disqualified for running for council because his company had done work for the school board and was still owned $2.35.

"That would make us beholden to him," they said.

Yes, that was petty, but petty is a large trait of those who are.

Fred cancelled the bill.

Later he was mayor, and became president of the Salmonbellies, the biggest, toughest lacrosse team anywhere, and he made it better by importing stars from the east and then winning the 1937 Mann Cup. He was so proud because back in the days when he was fixing toasters for seventy-five cents he played on the team, making nothing.

Enough of his statistics. The best thing, as I said, is that he was nice. He always had a smile, he always had something good to say about anyone he met and he remembered their names.

He quit politics to concentrate on the company he and Percy had made until it became the largest electrical supply house in western Canada.

Then his wife died and it was the only time I, or anyone else, saw that the unflinching smile was gone from his face. He later met another woman, Belva, who lived in the remote wilderness of West Vancouver and Fred moved there.

Now something happened that cannot happen. He was asked to run for mayor of Vancouver, without living there. First of all, there are no rules against it, but whoever heard of someone being mayor of a city they were not living in? No one ever, that's who. Second, he had already been mayor of New West. Whoever heard of doing it again? Again, no one.

Friendly Fred Hume was the only person to have been mayor of both New Westminster and Vancouver—and a member of the Hockey Hall of Fame.
Bill Cunningham photo, City of Vancouver Archives, AM54-S4-2-: CVA 371-2498

But he did, and during the campaign he never said a bad thing about the person he was running against. Whoever heard of that?

In fact, he never even mentioned his opponent's name.

He did something else no one had heard of. In an age when unions were being bashed by big business Fred said, "My firm has always been a union firm. We've got contracts now with seven unions."

And he won. Whoever heard of that?

They, meaning everyone, called him Friendly Fred.

This was also one of the fastest growing times of the city. A new Granville Street Bridge, the Oak Street Bridge. Also built was the Empire Stadium, for the race that would be called the Miracle Mile, where he the mayor smiled at the Queen.

This smiling kid who was born poor accepted only one dollar a year in pay during the eight years he was in office—the rest he gave to charity.

He was more than friendly.

FLYING PHIL

So he got three tickets. So what? So his licence was suspended a couple of times. He was in a hurry. He was serving God, and the people, and building roads and writing sermons and driving from Kamloops to Vancouver and then that ferry to Victoria.

That was slow.

And all the while the *Vancouver Sun* was attacking him. They did it so often readers looked at it like a continuing comic strip. He did this wrong, he did that wrong. If he did it, it was wrong.

Why, you ask? Such an easy answer. The *Sun* liked traditional politicians, basically English or Scottish background and boring. That's what the paper liked.

Phil Gaglardi was not boring. And he was ITALIAN. And he acted like one of them, they said. Impetuous, demonstrative, and he drove fast. How could someone like him be in government? But he was, and he was outstanding.

I remember riding with him when he pushed his car up to sixty miles per hour. The limit was fifty. And then the sirens.

"Do you know how fast you were going?" asked the constable on the motorcycle who knew how fast he was going.

"This is the speed we should all be driving," Phil said. "And I'm going to make it that way." He got the ticket and went on zooming south. And he pushed up the speed again. This was before seat belts so it was scary.

"Fifty is too slow," he said to me. "I made these roads and they're better than the famous ones in old Rome." In fact, he did make most of the roads. He was Minister of Highways in the 1950s when most of the roads in BC were built.

But there was so much more to Phil. He was born in Mission in 1913, one of eleven children of dirt poor Italian immigrants. Every time I look at immigrants now, from wherever they come from, struggling to survive, I say to myself they look like they have no future. And then I think of Phil.

He quit school at eight and took any job he could get, mostly digging ditches. But he looked at those big bulldozers and he said to me, "I wanted to drive them."

So he did. He squeezed in next to a driver and learned the gears and pedals and by the time he was fifteen he was driving them, for pay.

"When I order a road to be built I know it can be, because I could do it," he said. This was not the kind of politician the people of British Columbia were used to.

First thing after becoming the Minister of Highways was to increase the highway speed limit to sixty. Second thing he did was get a ticket for going over the limit.

"He's an embarrassment," the editors at the *Sun* said. And they said he built roads that were close to businesses run by friends and family. Okay, they had him on that one. But still the roads were built.

And he used some of them to get back to Kamloops each weekend so he could preach.

When he was driving bulldozers and living in logging and construction camps he did a bit of drinking and that led to a few brawls. Well, maybe more than a few.

He blamed his size for others starting them. He was only five foot four. And then he praised his size for winning the fights. "Don't mess with the short guy."

But things changed in his young twenties when he found God and went to a seminary in Seattle and was ordained at twenty-four. And he met Jennie Sandin in Kamloops, who was also a preacher. You know where that marriage was made.

Together they opened a church, your basic Pentecostal fire and brimstone church, in 1945. It had eight people come to pray. In less than ten years it grew and expanded and grew some more and they had 500 squeezing in for Sunday service.

Earlier I said he was writing his sermons, sometimes while flying behind his V8, and he was. But it was all in his head. All his sermons were ad-libbed. A half-hour off the top of his head: things you should fear, other things you should do, and don't get the two mixed up.

Then there were a series of radio sermons recorded for playing during the week. And finally, the Sunday school. He did not get much rest on the weekends, or the weekdays.

But what I liked most about Phil was the day he curved the highway.

This is a story that goes back a bit. There was a farmer named Charlie Perkins who ploughed his fields in a place called Langley. It wasn't a city, maybe it was a town, but all around it were farms. And one of them was Charlie's.

Then came World War I and Charlie said he should do his part. So after finishing putting the fields to bed for the winter, which he did with a horse and plough, he rode the horse to Vancouver, a full day's trip, and signed up.

Charlie was quite bright and he wound up as a pilot in the new air corps. He spent the next few years fighting in the sky, and amazing to everyone, including himself, he lived through it.

When he got back to his farm he planted a cedar tree where the corn was growing.

And time passed and the tree grew, as they have a habit of doing. He nailed all versions of the Canadian flag to it, the Maple Leaf and before the Maple Leaf. And he was at peace.

Then came the 1950s and the Trans-Canada Highway and one day Charlie looked at the horizon and saw surveyors aiming at him, and his tree.

Some of Charlie's family told me he did not have a shotgun. Some said of course he did. It does not matter. Charlie sat at the base of his tree and waited.

"You got to leave or we'll call the police," said the road crew.

"Not leaving," said Charlie.

"This is a big budget deal," said the crew. "We are going through."

"Go around it," said Charlie.

Well, they called the police and the same thing happened.

The police called Phil in his office in Kamloops. This part I can tell you about because I was in on it. I was visiting when the phone rang.

"What?!" said Phil. No, actually, "WHAT?!" shouted Phil.

I can tell you I would have hated to have been on the other end of that call. It was the foreman.

"It's going to cost more?" he said. "You said it will cost more to go around the tree?"

"Don't be an idiot. Go around the tree," Phil said loudly into the phone. You could hear him in the next room, or maybe down the street.

"So what if it costs more. Those men paid with their lives."

And that was the end of the call. There were no goodbyes. The road went around the tree and for the next sixty years there was a curve in Highway 1 just before 200th Street, and if you looked over to your right as you were going east you could see Charlie's tree.

Sadly, some idiot kids out for a night of drunken fun poured gasoline on the tree some years later. They set fire to it and killed the tree, so for most of those sixty years it was just a stump. Lucky for Charlie he was not alive to see it.

Then in the early 2010s the tall stump just gave up and came crashing down. The road has now been rebuilt and straightened. But if you drive by now you can see a miracle. Growing out of the base of the stump is a new tree.

All thanks to Charlie, and Phil.

There is just one other little thing I must mention because I am a thorough journalist and don't want to leave out any details, especially if they are juicy.

I am with Phil in his office having coffee and a sandwich for lunch and we finish and he says, "Pardon me, but could you leave me alone for a few minutes?"

Of course. I leave and outside I ask his secretary, "Important phone call?"

"No," she says sheepishly. "After lunch he takes off all his clothes and runs around his desk naked. It makes him feel free, he says."

Well, okay. We all have the things that make our lives exciting. But the *Vancouver Sun* did not know about that and I was not going to tell them. At least not until twenty-five years after he sped off on that highway to the sky, where there are no limits.

RICHARD CLEMENT MOODY

He really liked it here. He would have stayed, except for one little thing. I'll tell you about that later.

But first, Richard Clement Moody was my commanding officer and as such I give him the highest respect. He was a good officer. He was almost a friend, but not quite because an officer cannot be your friend. If he orders you to kill someone you have to do that. A friend would not order you to do it, an officer would.

But he was still good and kind and gentle. So I liked him. And he wanted to stay in British Columbia when all the hard work was done, but he didn't.

He was chosen for the job of settling this rugged, untamed land by Queen Victoria herself. Moody had already done well in the Falklands, which no one could find on any map. He settled that faraway land and brought law and order to it, and sheep. The sheep were important so that the British subjects on the remote island far off the coast of the south tip of South America would have something to keep them warm and something to eat.

The Queen liked that. She also liked that Richard Moody wanted to redesign Edinburgh Castle on the basis of musical chords. Please don't ask me

Richard Moody was constantly pushing expansion and more roads connecting New Westminster to other communities. At the time it was a pain, but looking back he built some of the foundations that help connect Lower Mainlanders to this day.

Image I-80338 courtesy of the Royal BC Museum and Archives

to explain that. But Moody was a gifted musician and a mathematician and he put those together and said he could build a better castle for the Queen.

You can see he was not an ordinary fellow.

But before he got around to renovating the castle, gold was discovered in British Columbia and the local head of the Hudson's Bay Company, James Douglas, called on the Queen to send help.

She sent Moody. He was the best of British culture and breeding. He was the archetypal British gentleman and British officer.

She gave him one order: "I want you to make a second England on the shores of the Pacific Ocean."

Well, that would be easy, or a challenge.

"Now go," she said.

Moody brought his wife Mary. She had more breeding and education than him. She was the highest of the high brow. For their honeymoon they went on a grand tour of Europe: France, Germany and Switzerland. Dancing and dinner every night. It was a marriage made in the highest aristocratic circles.

When they left for British Columbia six years later they had four children.

Mary did not like living here. It was backward. It was not like England. It was cold. And it rained a lot. And there was something else, that one little thing, which I'll tell you about down below.

But while she was writing to her sister about the drawbacks of BC her husband was building it. He told us Sappers to get busy. First, we had to build North Road. That would get the captains of the ships docking at Port Moody—"what a nice name, named after me," he said—to New Westminster to register their cargo.

Then we built Kingsway to connect the new remote capital of New West with the totally remote village of Gastown.

Except someone misjudged where Gastown was and when we got to what is now Main and Broadway someone said Gassy Jack is not here.

So we started another road hacking through the forest going straight north. That we called Westminster Highway. That would later be called Main Street, and that was to encourage Americans TO COME here, which is strange because our mission was to keep Americans FROM COMING here. You can never trust anyone's political motives.

I have been around long enough to see how Germany and Japan, which were America's number one enemies in World War II, are now America's major allies. Countries are like the people in them, and your relatives and friends and neighbours. They change. The lesson there is don't hold a grudge.

Anyway, we built a road and then another road to get us to Jack's saloon, which was nice because his beer tasted good.

But I was talking about Colonel Moody and the wonderful things he did.

He began construction—that was not him of course beginning construction, that was us—on the Cariboo Road just for the miners. Talk about your special interest group.

He set aside the land that would become Stanley Park as a military reserve to blast apart the Americans if they came that way, he named a lake in what would become Burnaby after his secretary Robert Burnaby (you read about him earlier and I hope you didn't skip that part), and there is some high land in what would become Port Coquitlam that he named after his wife, hence you have Mary Hill.

She was not impressed. She was having another baby. She did that a lot. She gave birth thirteen times in all, eleven lived.

But a bigger problem than Mary was that James Douglas, the offbeat, odd-looking giant who thought he was in charge of the whole shebang, did not like Moody. And Moody did not like Douglas. And they were both in charge of the same land.

Have you ever seen a boss and a second-in-command in the same company where the second-in-command had done all the work before the chosen one from outside was sent in to take over? You don't have to have seen it. You can imagine and you would be right.

Moody was pure English, whatever that meant, but it meant everything.

Douglas was what they called a "half-breed" back then—we would be banned from everywhere if we used that term now—born in the Caribbean, his father from Scotland and his mother, who was of mixed race herself, from Barbados. "Just look at him," they'd say. "He's not really white, and his wife, you know his wife, she's (pause) NATIVE." That meant everything, too.

Polite society in Victoria, over which Douglas was in charge, called him openly, "An affront to Victorian society. So good to have Colonel Moody in charge."

So the two of them did not have tea together.

And then came time for the mission of the Sappers to end. It had been nearly five years and there were other problems in the world.

Moody was asked if he wanted to return to England or retire in the new England, which was not quite finished being polished. He wanted to stay. He loved it here. He had already allotted an area almost four times the size of Stanley Park for himself. It was close to New Westminster. He was happy.

Mary was not. She wanted to go home with her four additional children and one more on the way. That was one for each year they were here. It was just that "other thing" that bothered her. When she learned that her

JAMES
Douglas

They will
cALL ME
The FATher
oF
BC

Richard
Moody

They will
cAll Me
The FATher
oF
BC

husband, this archetype of British culture, had two more children with their Indigenous housekeeper she was not amused.

He had been spending some late nights at the office.

So back they went to England, where he was promoted to general. Moody said he wanted to go back to BC. Who would not want to do that? Also he had some friends (a friend) here. He had left all his books behind.

But he died before he could get back. His books became the foundation of the New Westminster Library.

Just as a snarky aside, James Douglas did not have any children except with his wife.

MOODY ALSO, BUT LESS FAMOUS

It is confusing to have two earth-shaking people at almost the same time in almost the same place with the same name.

They were a decade apart and a half-day's boat ride followed by a full day's horse ride apart, but both were Moody and if you ask most people now about them you get: Moody? Don't know him. Two of them, you say? Nope. Don't know either.

That will teach anyone who thinks fame will follow them.

Moody One, that would be Richard, founded New Westminster and was given credit for founding BC. That is wrong, of course, it was James Douglas, but Moody was still the big shot. He also cheated on his wife.

Moody Two, that would be Sewell, founded a sawmill and died in a boating crash equal in its shock to the Titanic. He left behind a note that was surreal and scary.

Sewell Moody, thin, tall, dark and strong as a plank of Douglas fir, was called Sue. He travelled across the US by covered wagon with his family when he was fourteen. Think about it, walking three thousand miles because the less weight in the wagon was less on the horses. Then sleeping under the wagon hoping Native people who did not want you there would not come and kill you. Then waking and finding wood to make a fire to boil water to cook the beans in, again, so you would have strength to walk all day, again.

And while you walked you were wondering why and where you were going. Your father said there was a future in the West but you were happy with your life in the back alley next to your old home in the East.

Then more walking and without making it sound as tedious and scary and mindless as it was you were there on the west coast.

And like a fourteen-year-old he asked, "So what do we do now?"

And his father looked at him and said, "We will start a new life."

Well, okay, Sue wasn't doing anything else at the moment.

The teen years pass and he ends up in BC learning the work of the forest, mostly measuring the giant trees by sight and estimating how much they would be worth when cut. It was a special craft and you had to be right because the mills would buy logs based on your numbers.

If you were wrong you could go and cut the trees yourself, which would rip out your arms and back and possibly kill you. Better to be right.

I met Sue when he was about twenty-eight. We went by boat across Burrard Inlet to a dilapidated sawmill on the north shore he had heard about.

"What do you think?" he asked me.

This was 1862, long before I died. I could only see massive hard work ahead for him, more than I wanted to do. The good thing was the forest came right to the edge of the water. You could cut the trees and they would basically fall right outside the mill.

Another good thing was there were so many trees, the forest was so thick, Moody would never run out of supply. It was just there waiting for him.

The bad thing was: who would cut the trees and who would work the mill?

"If it works you will do well," I said. "If you can't you'll be sitting on a lot of trees and a lot of debt, which might kill you."

He laughed. "I'm buying it."

He and a partner, Moses Ireland (what a great name, the Bible and the emerald island together), chipped in together and got it for a song. Those were his words. I hoped someone would not do the same to him in a few years.

Now here's what happened. I'll give it to you quickly with no build up.

Men came to work and a company town grew. Sue had a puritanical streak and ran the town and mill with a firm hand. There was no alcohol and no gambling.

Soon the men brought wives and Sue opened a school and held religious services. Then he opened a library and a reading room for the times when his workers were not working. He built the first Masonic Lodge on Burrard Inlet, then extended the telegraph line from New Westminster. He paid for that himself.

The second teacher to arrive, Margaret Thain, had credentials from Britain, which was more than most other teachers in the province. But there was something the town did not have.

"I don't want to work in a place with no name," Margaret said. "We will call it Moodyville." And thus it was, officially.

As for business, the Moodyville sawmill became the largest single source of export revenue in British Columbia. The wood was so good it was known around the world. First, the beams were huge, and second, there were no knots in them. It was pure, iron strong wood. And it went to China, South America, Australia and Europe. At times there were a half-dozen giant sailing ships waiting in the inlet to load.

Then came the day Sewell Moody had to go to San Francisco on business. California wanted his wood. He sailed to Victoria and spent some time with his wife, Janet Watson. They had been married six years and had two children.

He kissed Janet goodbye before dawn on November 4, 1869, and boarded the steamer *Pacific*. It was a giant of a paddlewheeler that had served on both coasts, sometimes carrying passengers and freight and sometimes as a cruise ship to Hawaii. In first class there were cabins and a fancy dining room. In steerage there was room to sleep below decks and a place to eat.

There were 275 paying passengers, but just as the gates closed a few dozen more pushed their way through without tickets, which often happened. They could easily avoid being caught during the three-day trip. Also children went free and were not counted, so no one knows how many were on board.

Just out of Victoria the ship ran into a storm and started listing. To straighten it the crew filled the life boats on one side with water.

Later that night a larger sailing ship was going north. The captain had gone below and left control in the hands of his first mate with instructions that if you see a light turn west. It will be the Cape Flattery lighthouse.

In the pitch blackness the mate saw a light. He turned west. The light was from the *Pacific*. They scraped sides, almost a casual bump, and the sailing ship was unhurt except for losing some rigging. The Pacific was gouged, and kept going and sinking.

The crew of the sailing ship was angry that the steamer did not stop to see if they needed help. Unknown to them in the darkness the steamer had already gone down. The lifeboats were useless. Only two survivors. They reported that the ocean was filled with screams that soon went silent.

Just before he fell into the sea Sewell Moody got a broken piece of wood and wrote his name on it, and "all is lost." Two weeks later that piece of wood floated up on a beach near Victoria.

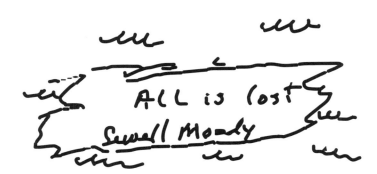

It was brought to his wife.

The boy named Sue was not a romantic, but he was a good man, and he left his mark.

Moodyville continued to thrive for another ten years but by then the trees that had no end were coming to an end.

The mill slowed and then closed. The town struggled on but in 1924 a wonderful, terrible thing happened. Progress. A bridge was built across the inlet. It was the Second Narrows Bridge, but not the one you see today, which is now the Ironworkers Memorial Bridge. This was the first Second Narrows.

It brought cars and trains and then the grain elevators could be built to sell another Canadian product. Then a road was built from the bridge along the waterfront next to the tracks, which were next to the grain elevators.

The road and the tracks went right through Moodyville. Nothing was left, no sawmill, no building, nothing.

All was lost.

Every time I drive on the Low Level Road I nod my head to Sue.

ASAHI
BASEBALL

The thing was, they could not win. Oh, they won sometimes and they were great players, but really they were no match against the white guys. There was one thing the white guys had that they did not and that was a lot of whiteness covering a lot of body. In short, those white guys were big and the little brown guys were not.

Excuse me. I know we don't use racial slurs any longer, and that is good. In fact that is better than good, it is a miracle. It took less than three hundred years in America just to get people to recognize that names do more than hurt, they demoralize and ruin lives.

Canada was a little behind because it was not that old. But we are talking about the *Vancouver Sun* and the *Daily Province*, which would cover baseball games and report on the "Japs" or the "Nips" and no one, except those getting demeaned, thought anything about it.

I loved watching the games at the Powell Street Grounds. You know it as Oppenheimer Park, which is now a sad plot of mud and fences meant to keep people out. The fences come and go depending on where the homeless pitch their tents. It is so sad. The park, the homeless, the garbage, the lack of a place for families go and kids to play. But for now, baseball.

I, along with crowds standing shoulder to shoulder, would stand outside the fence that was there only to protect us from foul balls, and would cheer and groan and cheer and groan while our Asahi bunted their way around the bases.

Yes, bunted. That was the secret that made the Asahi one of the greatest teams of all time.

The Japanese living in Japantown loved baseball. We all loved baseball. There was no football. We knew how it was played, but no one here did. Throwing a ball back and forth and then banging into someone. What skill is that?

Baseball was skill.

There was no soccer. No one here had ever heard of it. And there was no basketball. It existed on the East Coast, but East was East and this was the West and we played baseball. That sounds like an iron-clad reason enough for me.

But what do you do when the other teams outweigh your team by fifty pounds for each player? And they are sluggers, and you are not. And they get home runs, and you don't.

Tell me, what do you do when it is impossible to win? Once again, that impossible word is there just to be a target. You get a team manager who says, "Impossible? Never."

He was Harry Miyasaki, who was even shorter than most of his players. But he said that was not a problem. He would use his head, his brain, his imagination. He told me about watching Japanese and Chinese martial arts, where size was not a factor.

"You use your opponent's weight against him," he said.

"In baseball?" I was confused. "You don't touch the other players. Or you will be thrown out."

Harry told me to come their practice that summer evening when the sun was up late.

"No swinging, no hitting," Harry told his players. "We bunt."

He had them practice bunting for an hour. That is long time to hold a baseball bat and not swing it.

"Can we hit just once?" asked a player.

"No, because you can't hit it over the fence and they can."

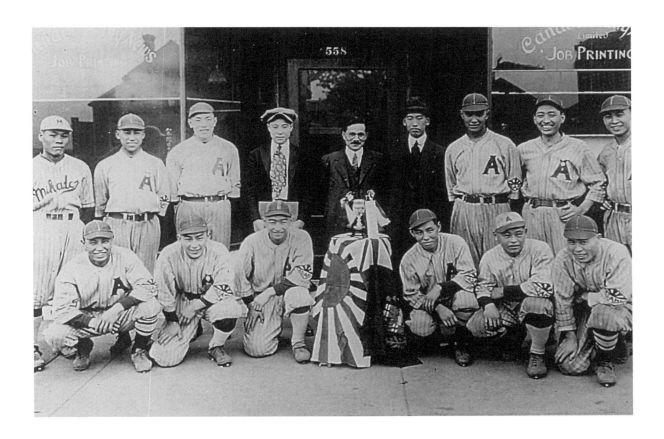

Bunt. Bunt to second base. Bunt until the ball stops in front of the pitcher. Bunt until you can pick a spot, any spot, and make it yours.

That was half of Harry's plan. They slug, we bunt.

And then: steal. "We are fast, at least we are faster than most of them. And we can steal when we bunt."

They practiced every night with martial discipline. They practiced until they played as one. And they practiced the signals. When the third base coach signalled to go from second to third the runner went. There was no hesitation, deliberation or wondering if it was the right call.

And then they developed "Otose." The Japanese word that meant "drop it" or "bunt."

The Japanese-Canadian Asahi Baseball Club won numerous tournaments and championships before being broken up during World War II.

Harbour Publishing Archives

219

When the first base coach yelled "Otose" the players were running before the ball hit the bat. They could sometimes get two runners across the plate on one pitch.

This was baseball like no one had ever seen. The newspapers called it "brain ball" or "smart ball." But the newspapers still used the names Nips and Japs and Little Brown Men. But the newspapers also had to report the scores, which less and less went to the big white men.

And there was one game, in 1928, when the Asahi beat the other team 3 to 1. However, the Asahi never had a hit. They did it all with walks, sacrifice bunts, steals and not making errors like the other team did over and over trying to pick up the bunts.

And then came December 7, 1941, and the bunts and steals were over. Sad, painful. Most of the players brought their gloves and bats with them to the camps, but they were not together, and that was the day the most wonderful baseball ever played died.

BABE RUTH

It was October 20, 1934, and I was sitting on a board in the bleachers and I was soaked. It was not raining, it was pouring. And what am I doing in a ball park in the rain? No, in the pouring rain?

That is stupid.

But Babe Ruth was coming and I would not mind getting drenched right down to my underwear, which I already was, to see the Babe swing a bat.

He had arrived the day before with his wife and daughter on the fancy ship the *Empress of Japan*. It was not raining then. He and other baseball greats, dubbed the All-Americans, were going to Japan to play some exhibition games.

But the next day, the day after that, this day that was filled with rain, they were scheduled to play in Vancouver. I bought a ticket. The ticket was between my fingers. It was soggy.

Babe Ruth was not the king of home runs. Heck anyone great and unbeatable could be that. Babe Ruth was the celestial emperor of the Empire of Home Runs. He was the most well-known person on earth.

And now he was going to play one game in Athletic Park, which was near False Creek, near Fifth and Granville.

But it was pouring and everyone said, "No game. Stay in the hotel and stay dry." But I was sitting here, and others were sitting here, 3,000 of us were sitting here in the rain hoping the Babe would show up.

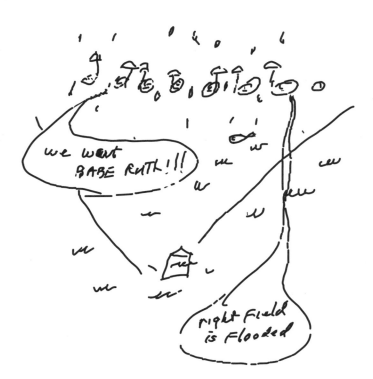

we want BABE RUTH!!!

right field is flooded

Word of us got to him in the Hotel Vancouver where he was staying in the Royal Suite, and smoking a pipe and sipping on brandy. And he said—these are immortal words because they were spoken by an immortal being: "IF THESE PEOPLE CAN TAKE THE WEATHER SO CAN WE. WE'RE GOING TO GIVE THEM A BALL GAME."

He got on his Yankees uniform and headed through the pounding rain to the park. Would any other hero do as much? Now you understand the adoration of Babe Ruth, a kid who grew up in a reformatory. Whatever he did wrong when he was young was wrong. But he threw a baseball and that

Babe Ruth was so famous that crowds would gather at the slightest rumour of a sighting. He's the one between the two women—his wife and daughter—if you couldn't tell.

Stuart Thomson photo, City of Vancouver Archives, AM1535-: CVA 99-5051

was enough. He rose above the impossible to rise above his past and he reached the top.

And then rain came, and to us he stayed on top.

When he climbed out of the dugout we cheered and cheered and did some more.

By the third inning he and the other players were soaked right down to the skin under their underwear. We in the stands had umbrellas and waterproof coats. We lived here. But not the Bambino.

He was soaked right through. In the dugout we could see he took off his cap and wrung it out. As a joke the first baseman came out with an umbrella. Maybe it wasn't a joke.

Babe did knock two balls out of the stadium, but they went foul. Those balls probably went on to help some kids get a month of groceries. There were many balls circulating around after the game that had Babe's signature. Only two did he actually touch.

Just as an aside, the only player who did not look so good was the catcher. Turned out he was actually a spy sent on the trip by the US government to get information about Japan. Home movies that he shot of the Tokyo skyline were used after the bombing of Pearl Harbor in the retaliatory bombing of Tokyo.

Back to that game in the rain. It ended in a tie, which never happens in baseball. But they were too wet to keep playing.

Then the All-Americans continued on their way to Japan. And the stadium was knocked down to make a northbound on-ramp for the Granville Bridge.

223

But most of all Babe Ruth played in Vancouver, and that was a home run for the city, no matter how dripping wet the memory was.

Babe Ruth playing here in the rain. That's impossible. But you know about that word.

So many amazingly wonderful people have lived here, people with stories that could change the lives of others. They are our heritage. And someday someone will probably write stories about you, possibly me.

But now, it is time for another nap.